DATE DUE

GAYLORD   PRINTED IN U.S.A.

Marie-Claire Blais

Mary Jean Green

Dartmouth College

Twayne Publishers
An Imprint of Simon & Schuster Macmillan
New York

Prentice Hall International
London • Mexico City • New Delhi • Singapore • Sydney • Toronto

Library
University of Texas
at San Antonio

Marie-Claire Blais
Mary Jean Green

Copyright © 1995 by Twayne Publishers

Twayne Publishers
An Imprint of Simon & Schuster Macmillan
866 Third Avenue
New York, NY 10022

Library of Congress Cataloging-in-Publication Data

Green, Mary Jean Matthews.
    Marie-Claire Blais / Mary Jean Green.
        p. cm. — (Twayne's world authors series; TWAS 856)
    Includes bibliographical references and index.
    ISBN 0-8057-4547-5 (alk. paper)
1. Blais, Marie-Claire—Criticism and interpretation. I. Title. II. Series.
PQ3919.B6Z68 1995
843'—dc20   94-44449
                                                                     CIP

10 9 8 7 6 5 4 3 2 1

Printed in the United States of America.

To my son Matthew,
who has come to share my love for Quebec

Contents

Preface

When she was barely 20, Marie-Claire Blais was recognized in Quebec for the penetrating poetic vision of her writing, and her literary reputation quickly spread to the United States and France. The originality of her early works, with their dreamlike mythical settings, gave way to greater realism and a fluid narrative voice that lends itself to a critical yet compassionate analysis of the modern world. At times shocked by her somber vision of the human condition and the state of the contemporary world, Blais's readers have been moved by her sympathetic portrayal of suffering human beings in their search for relationships and love.

Blais's work undergoes radical shifts in subject matter and style with every new publication, and it thus resists attempts to encompass it within a single critical account. The biting satire of traditional Quebec she undertook in *Une saison dans la vie d'Emmanuel* made her a favorite of the young intellectuals of Quebec's Quiet Revolution and suggested a political interpretation of her early Freudian fairy tale, *La Belle Bête*. Feminist readers, on the other hand, have privileged her sympathetic portrayal of Montreal lesbian communities in *Les Nuits de l'Underground,* as well as the moving studies of mothers and daughters that fill the pages of *Visions d'Anna.* The vague poetic landscapes of *Le Jour est noir* evoked a different response, and yet another was called forth by the scathing satire of Quebec intellectual circles portrayed in *Un Joualonais sa Joualonie.* And her portrait of the artist as a young girl, *Manuscrits de Pauline Archange,* has entered the canon of Francophone autobiography.

Blais has refused to enlist her writing in the service of any cause, yet she has written of the omnipresent danger of war, the lives of the homeless, the devastation of AIDS, the desperation of young drug addicts. She has maintained a discreet silence about her personal life, yet she has written movingly about the experience of poverty in Quebec and of women's lives on the margins of social convention. The Marie-Claire Blais with whom I have had personal contact is shy, sensitive, and warmly responsive to those around her, yet some of her works suggest another vision— a writer who is passionate, darkly pessimistic, and drawn to situations of violence.

Each of Blais's writings creates its own world of reality and calls for a different mode of reading. Her work resists a critic's attempt to create structures that would contain it, patterns that would define its evolution. Yet texts separated by many years return to earlier themes and continue to explore central aspects of human experience. I have arranged my study of Blais's work in rough chronological order, devoting separate chapters to those I consider to be her major novels: *La Belle Bête, Une saison dans la vie d'Emmanuel, Le Sourd dans la ville, Visions d'Anna.* Her other novels are grouped according to their focus on various themes: the life of the couple, the alienation of adolescence, love among women. In one case—that of the humorous satires of contemporary intellectual life that punctuate her work in the mid-1970s—the unity is not only thematic but stylistic as well. In addition to her work as a novelist, Blais has written a number of plays for the stage, radio, and television, and these dramatic works, written over a span of 25 years, have been grouped together in a single chapter. Such categories and groupings are necessitated by the nature of the critical genre within which I am working, but I have nevertheless tried to respect the autonomy of the individual work.

More than is true in the case of other writers, each of Blais's readers has a different vision of her. While I have tried to take into account the variety of responses her writing has evoked, the Marie-Claire Blais who is the subject of this book is, in large part, the creation of my own passionately engaged reading.

Acknowledgments

I would like to thank the Government of Quebec for a summer research grant that permitted me to begin gathering the documentation for this book. Thanks is also due to Dartmouth College for its continuing research support. I am grateful to Marie Couillard, who called to my attention the collection of Blais's working notebooks housed in the National Library of Canada, and to Claude LeMoyne, whose dedication to preserving the work of Canadian writers has made these important documents available to scholars. I thank my colleagues and fellow Blais scholars Paula Gilbert Lewis, Karen Gould, Victor-Laurent Tremblay, Marie Couillard, and Janine Ricouart for making available to me the results of their research and for their helpful comments on parts of my own work. My general editor, David O'Connell. has provided much helpful criticism and advice, and I have appreciated the patient guidance of Anne Kiefer, my editor in New York. Finally, I am grateful to Marie-Claire Blais for her kind words of encouragement as I undertook this project.

Chronology

1972   *Le Loup.*

1973   *Un Joualonais sa Joualonie.*

1974   *Fièvre et autres textes dramatiques.*

1975   Returns to Quebec, dividing her time between a village in the Eastern Townships and Montreal.

1976   *Une liaison parisienne.* Contributes monologue to feminist dramatic production, *La Nef des sorcières.*

1977   *L'Océan suivi de murmures* (dramatic texts).

1978   *Les Nuits de l'Underground.*

1979   *Le Sourd dans la ville,* which receives the Governor General's award.

1980   *Visions d'Anna.*

1982   Is awarded the Prix Athanase David in Quebec for her life's work.

1983   Receives Prix de l'Académie Française in France for *Visions d'Anna.*

1984   *Pierre, ou la guerre du printemps 81* and *Sommeil d'hiver* (dramatic texts).

1987   *Le Sourd dans la ville* is adapted for film by director Mireille Dansereau.

1988   Play *L'Ile* is produced in Montreal by Théâtre de l'Eskabel.

1989   *L'Ange de la solitude.*

1993   Publication of autobiographical essays, *Parcours d'un écrivain: Notes américaines.*

Chapter One
A Writer's Odyssey

With the publication in 1959 of *La Belle Bête* by the 20-year-old Marie-Claire Blais, the Quebec literary world discovered a young writer whose dark world of haunting obsessions represented a new voice in the Quebec novelistic tradition. "[T]he writing of this extraordinary young woman is so individual, so unlike anything else being written on this continent," wrote Robertson Davies a few years later in the *New York Times Book Review*.[1] Interviewers flocked to a studio apartment in the narrow, history-laden streets of Quebec City to find a shy young writer who claimed to draw her monstrous fictional characters from her own imagination. *La Belle Bête,* appearing on the eve of the sweeping process of political and social change in Quebec that would become known as the Quiet Revolution, already pointed toward the forces that would touch off an explosion of creative energy in the Quebec literature of the 1960s. Five years after the publication of her first novel, Blais's biting satire of traditional rural Quebec in *Une saison dans la vie d'Emmanuel* would drive the final nail in the coffin of an outmoded literary vision and would establish itself as a classic of this new literary movement.

The eminent critic Edmund Wilson, who was to become Blais's literary mentor, praised her first four novels as "remarkable books of a passionate and poetic force that . . . is not otherwise to be found in French Canadian fiction."[2] Wilson noted that these works were not even set in Quebec, yet for him they reflected the deep reality of the literature of French Canada, capable of reaching beyond its borders: "her work has more than local interest. It is the refinement to a purer kind of poetry than that of the protesting patriots of the desperate cry that arises from the poverty, intellectual and material, the passionate self-punishing piety and the fierce defeated pride of Quebec" (Wilson, 153–54).

Marie-Claire Blais was born in Quebec City in 1939 to a family of modest means.[3] Although she remained an only child for seven years, by the time she was in her teens the house was filled with the activity of her four younger brothers and sisters. Her father worked as an engineer, but the family's resources were stretched by the necessity of providing for five children, and they were unable to subsidize their eldest daughter's literary career, which they feared would not provide her with a living. The atmosphere of Blais's childhood, if not its actual events, is evoked in her trilogy of the late 1960s, *Manuscrits de Pauline Archange,* in which she describes a young girl who affirms her vocation as a writer against the oppressive social forces of Quebec in the 1950s. In a French-speaking Canadian province dominated by a rigid and monolithic Catholic church, writers were censored, and all expressions of sexuality were strictly repressed.

Blais herself began writing very young, beginning her first novel at the age of nine and staging theatrical productions with her younger siblings. In *Manuscrits de Pauline Archange* one of these performances is broken up by the girl's father in an attempt to reclaim his prized beaver hat, which has been serving as a prop. By the time she was in high school, Blais was spending several hours a day at her typewriter. Nevertheless, she was forced to cut short her secondary education at the Convent of St. Roch in order to undergo a year of secretarial training, after which she took a series of office jobs—nine in the space of a few years—all of which she heartily disliked. The solitude felt by Pauline Archange as she was abruptly cut off from her studies, as well as her inability to concentrate on the mundane tasks of the working world, must certainly reflect Blais's experience of those years.

Despite the demands of earning a living, Blais made time for her writing. Her independent income enabled her to move out of her family's home, where the necessity of sharing a bedroom with two younger sisters made it impossible for her to work at her typewriter. After moving to a room near the old Laval University campus, she was able to devote the time left free from her various jobs to the feverish production of manuscripts.

At this time she also enrolled in evening classes at the university and made two contacts there that would change her life. Jeanne Lapointe, Laval's first woman professor of literature, had used her position to encourage women writers, among them Anne Hébert. Lapointe immediately recognized the genius in Blais's early manuscripts and worked closely with her in preparing them for publication. Her second academic mentor was Father Georges-Henri Lévesque, who, as head of social sciences at Laval, had been largely responsible for the modernization of the university's curriculum. At the time Blais met him, he was vice president of the Council of Arts. After looking over his young visitor's briefcase full of manuscripts, Father Lévesque reportedly asked her to produce a simple, coherent work. Two weeks later Blais brought him the manuscript of *La Belle Bête,* which she had written in a burst of intense activity, and Lévesque immediately took it to a publisher.

On the heels of the success of her first novel, Blais moved to Montreal, where she found more enjoyable employment in the judicial archives, and in 1961 she won a Canada Council grant, which enabled her to spend a year in France. Her early novels drew her the attention of Edmund Wilson, who met her as he researched his book on contemporary Canadian writers, *O Canada,* in which Blais was to figure prominently. Because of Wilson's encouragement, Blais applied for a Guggenheim fellowship, and in 1963 she left Quebec for the United States to spend a year in the university atmosphere of Cambridge, Massachusetts.

Blais's life in Cambridge was often lonely; her notebooks record her feeling of isolation from the privileged Harvard students whom she observed lounging on the lawns of their well-kept campus. But it did provide the occasion for her meeting and ensuing close relationship with the artist Mary Meigs, a neighbor of Wilson's on Cape Cod. In her autobiography, Meigs warmly recalls her first encounter with Blais, a visit to Harvard's Fogg Museum of Art, during which the younger woman plied her with questions about literature.[4] Blais recalls Mary Meigs's mention of the series of self-portraits in which she was engaged, and her evocation of a life in which each hour of the day was devoted to poetry, painting, or music.[5] This conjunction of literature and art was an appropriate introduction to the life they were to lead together on Cape Cod, when Blais moved into a small house in Wellfleet near the one Meigs shared with the antiwar activist Barbara Deming. Even in the avant-gardist intellectual community of Wellfleet, the sight of two independent women living together without a man was seen as a shocking provocation, and Blais was attracted by their refusal to submit to a conformist society.

The Wellfleet years, which extended from 1964 to 1969, were an important time of apprenticeship for Blais, as she has recorded in the detailed notebooks she kept during that time. While she had drawn the material of her early novels primarily from her own nightmarish imagination, she now began to devour the world's great literature. Cambridge bookstores sent her piles of Proust, Balzac, Camus, James, Tolstoy, Dostoyevski, Flaubert, and Virginia Woolf, in addition to current novels from Quebec. Blais also began to experiment with painting, showing what Meigs has described as a natural talent. Meigs's judgment finds its confirmation in the paintings and drawings that spill out of Blais's notebooks from those years—scenes of Wellfleet competing with abstract designs drawn from Matisse and Picasso and black and white sketches of her own fictional characters. Blais also devoted a part of her day's schedule to listening to classical music, a sustained interest that accounts for the many musical references in her work. What Meigs has described as the "Puritan discipline" of days devoted to these alternating intellectual pursuits was lightened by social evenings with Edmund and Elena Wilson and other members of the Wellfleet intellectual community and by occasional visits to Quebec to launch a new book.

Blais's life in Wellfleet was also darkened by her sensitivity to world events. Although she could not share Barbara Deming's role in active antiwar protest, she worried about her friend's vulnerability, especially when on several occasions Deming was arrested and imprisoned. In her memoirs, *Parcours d'un écrivain,* Blais recalls her first meeting with Barbara as she emerged from a 30-day fast in a Birmingham, Alabama, prison, the experience that would be the source of her influential book *Prison Notes.* While Blais and Meigs were shocked by the pacifist's emaciated form, Deming herself was strengthened by her commitment and the support of the women who shared her emprisonment:

> Elle a écrit dans cette prison de Birmingham son livre *Prison Notes* qui sera beaucoup lu par les futures générations de pacifistes et de résistants non violents; c'est aussi le journal d'une révolutionnaire, d'une mystique qui croit à la prière et au jeûne, le récit d'une expérience de solidarité avec d'autres compagnons de lutte, dans l'amour et la privation. [In that Birmingham prison she wrote her book *Prison Notes,* which will be much read by future generations of pacifists and nonviolent resistants; it is also the journal of a revolutionary, a mystic who believes in prayer and fasting, the story of an experience of solidarity with other comrades, in love and deprivation.] (*Parcours,* 101)

In her recollection of Deming as "l'amie révolutionnaire," Blais marvels at her mysterious determination to sacrifice her peaceful life with her friends, motivated by "un humanisme patient, rigoureux qui me semblait souvent incompréhensible"[6] [a patient, rigorous humanism that often seemed incomprehensible to me].

Blais herself grew increasingly concerned about the violence and unrest surrounding the American war in Vietnam, an atmosphere that slowly finds its way into her fictional universe, particularly the darkly oppressive *David Sterne.* Her notebooks record her feeling of the impossibility of being an artist in a world headed toward destruction, where everything seems criminal and all action meaningless.[7] At other moments, however, she saw her writing as the only possible response:

> Comment écrire autre chose que l'injustice ressentie quand on vit dans une atmosphère si chargée de rumeurs de guerre, de brutalité, de racisme aussi outrageusement exprimé? J'essaie pourtant d'écrire tous les jours, et ce geste me paraît le seul geste décent et utile que je puisse accomplir. [How can I write about anything other than the injustice you feel when you live in an atmosphere so filled with rumblings of war, brutality, and racism expressed so outrageously? I try nevertheless to write every day, and that seems to me the only decent, useful thing I can do.] (*Parcours,* 66)

It was while she was in Wellfleet, far from the oppressive realities of traditional Quebec, that Blais wrote *Une saison dans la vie d'Emmanuel,* the novel that firmly established her place in the Quebec literary canon. While *La Belle Bête* had attracted the attention of North American critics, this satiric depiction of rural Quebec made Blais's reputation in France, receiving the prestigious Prix Médicis in 1966, along with the adulation of critics. The French reveled in the picturesque nature of its Canadian setting, but Quebec readers joyously responded to its biting attack on a tradition-bound Quebec that was even then beginning to give way to the groundswell of the Quiet Revolution, making Blais a heroine of Quebec's young intellectuals.

The novels she wrote while living in Quebec had been set in vaguely outlined poetic worlds, but her self-imposed exile in the United States seemed to give her the perspective she needed to write about her own experience. It was in Cambridge and Wellfleet that Blais undertook the more realistic treatment of her own Quebec childhood—the three volumes of *Manuscrits de Pauline Archange*—which initiated a period in which her writing was permeated by autobiographical elements and became increasingly sensitive to events in the world around her.

The success of *Une saison dans la vie d'Emmanuel* led Blais to spend more and more time in France and, at the urging of a French friend, Blais and Meigs (who were no longer living with Deming) decided to transfer their lives from the United States to France, re-creating their Cape Cod retreat in a farmhouse in Brittany. Although she continued to maintain a quiet rural base, Blais's life at this time became less sedentary, and she began to divide her time between her Breton solitude and the activity of Paris and Montreal. This period of her life forms the background for her satiric novel, *Une liaison parisienne,* where she records her disillusionment with the glitter of Parisian literary life and her respect for the simple humanity of the Breton farmers.

When she returned definitively to Quebec in 1975, she found it, as she told Margaret Atwood, "a far different place: vibrant, alive, a good place to be."[8] This positive view of Quebec is shared by her artist-protagonist Geneviève in *Les Nuits de l'Underground,* a novel in which Blais wrote freely, for the first time, about the experiences of a lesbian. Although never a militant for any cause, Blais displayed her solidarity with Quebec's growing feminist movement by contributing a short dramatic monologue, "Marcelle," also focusing on lesbian experience, to the landmark feminist project organized by fellow writers Nicole Brossard and France Théoret, the collective dramatic production entitled *La Nef des sorcières.*

Blais continued to maintain a home in the country, eventually settling in a rural writers' colony in Quebec's Eastern Townships, but spent much of her time absorbing the varied cosmopolitan atmosphere of urban Montreal, which becomes a privileged setting of her novels, especially the important landmarks of her mature work, *Le Sourd dans la ville* and *Visions d'Anna.* Although these novels seem to offer the hope of human contact, Blais's vision of the world has become increasingly apocalyptic in works like *Pierre,* about youthful violence, and *L'Ile,* a play set on an island whose population is being slowly destroyed by the epidemics of the modern world. The setting of *L'Ile* is also a transposition of another place in which Blais has found a spiritual home and a respite from the Quebec winters that menace her early protagonists. In her 1993 memoirs she writes of her contacts with the writers and artists who constitute the community of Key West, from internationally known authors like John Hersey to old women who will never publish their works. At home in a world of tropical sun that is in every way remote from the cold, oppressive atmosphere of her childhood, Blais continues to observe and identify with marginal beings, the stray cats who wander into the home of the late novelist Ernest Hemingway, the fortune-teller who preserves memories of Tennessee Williams's fragile sister, the young couple who sing and play at the bar.

Blais's preeminent position in the Quebec literary world is shared with only a handful of other writers, among them her much-admired contemporaries Réjean Ducharme (to whom she dedicated *Manuscrits de Pauline Archange)* and Anne Hébert. Her work has been recognized by a number of literary prizes in France and Quebec, including the Governor General's award for *Manuscrits de Pauline Archange* and *Le Sourd dans la ville,* and the Prix Médecis and the Prix de l'Académie Française for *Visions d'Anna.* Two of her novels, *Une saison dans la vie d'Emmanuel* and *Le Sourd dans la ville,* have been made into films. Although she is best known as a novelist, she has had several plays produced in Montreal and has also published collections of poetry. While each of her works is a new beginning, often representing a radical departure from its predecessor in terms of subject matter and style, the underlying themes of human suffering and solitude continue to assert their presence, just as Blais herself retains the gentle shyness that has fascinated interviewers from the time of her first youthful publication.

Chapter Two

A Tale of Many Meanings:
La Belle Bête

La Belle Bête (Mad Shadows), published when Blais was barely 20, brought her immediately into the literary spotlight in her own province and beyond. As I have noted, the short novel was written in the space of two weeks in response to the request of her intellectual mentor, Father Georges-Henri Lévesque, for a coherent work, "a clear, simple story."[1] While some readers found its unchained passions and family violence a sign of "immoralisme,"[2] important critics like Gilles Marcotte immediately recognized Blais's poetic gifts. The young author shyly received interviewers in her one-room apartment and expressed her dream of living in Paris. *La Belle Bête* was discovered by the visiting American critic Edmund Wilson, who called it "a story of country life that is in its narrower way as . . . shocking as Zola's" (Wilson, 148), which helped win her a Guggenheim fellowship that eventually allowed her to take up residence in the United States.

Striking in its dense poetry and primordial violence, *La Belle Bête* has given rise to numerous, often contradictory readings. In the vagueness of its setting and the unidimensionality of its characters, as well as in many explicit references, the novel consciously situates itself in a world of myth and fairy tale. By its focus on a family in an agricultural setting it also suggests its link with the literary tradition of Quebec rural novels, which, in the 1950s, were only beginning to be displaced by more contemporary forms.

Events move quickly in this short tale of violence and death. The story opens on the family constituted by the widowed Louise and her two children, the angelically beautiful but mindless Patrice and the ugly but intelligent Isabelle-Marie. Refusing to recognize Patrice's idiocy, Louise idolizes her son, in whom she sees a reflection of her own beauty, while totally rejecting her daughter. Nonetheless, Isabelle-Marie carries on the work of the dead father by running the family farms. In a situation guaranteed to engender sibling rivalry, a reaction is not long in coming, for, as several critics have noted, these characters tend to act out the normally repressed desires of the unconscious.[3] While her mother is away on a trip, Isabelle-Marie withholds food from her brother, nearly starving him to death. When Louise returns with Lanz, her new husband, it is Patrice's turn to act out his jealousy, finally running down his rival with a horse, in a quintessentially Oedipal scene.

Meanwhile, Isabelle-Marie has found happiness with a blind neighbor, Michaël, who has no reason to doubt her false claims to beauty. But when he miraculously regains his sight, Michaël rejects both Isabelle-Marie and their baby daughter, Anne, in whom Isabelle-Marie's ugliness is reflected. Forced to return to the scene of her unhappy childhood, Isabelle-Marie takes her final revenge on her brother by plunging his face into boiling water. Since he is no longer beautiful, Louise packs him off to an asylum. As a final act of revolt, Isabelle-Marie sets fire to the farm, in the process killing her mother, who is already being consumed by a cancerous growth that disfigures her face. Abandoning her daughter, Isabelle-Marie throws herself under a train, and Patrice, returning to find his home in ashes, drowns by plunging himself into the lake in a vain attempt to reunite with his once-beautiful image.

As this final scene is clearly a reenactment of the Narcissus myth, the events of the plot evoke elements of myth and fairy tale. Patrice's murder of his stepfather in order to restore his exclusive relationship with his mother is clearly a repetition of the Oedipus story, while the family configuration of usurping stepfather, rejected daughter loyal to the father, and avenging son suggests the brother-sister plot of Orestes and Electra. Many of the same unhappy family constellations occur in the world of fairy tale. The mother preoccupied with her own beauty who rejects her daughter is reminiscent of the evil queen of Snow White, and the mother's unjust persecution of the true daughter of the father links her to the cruel stepmother of Cinderella. The relationship to the world of myth and fairy tale is emphasized by the distanced tone of the omniscient narration and its reinforcement of stereotyped modes of representation, particularly the image of woman as witch.

In her overlaid references to various intertexts, Blais creates a polysemous text that leaves much room for interpretation. If the plot is "simple," its meaning is anything but "clear." Gilles Marcotte, who pointed out the poetic form of this novel, also recognized the way in which its young author had forced her readers to abandon traditional modes of interpretation: "It breaks out of our rules, not only by the precocity of expression it reveals . . . but also, and especially, because it mixes genres with a stupefying and irreproachable freedom."[4] While noting the novel's link to the *conte fantastique*, Marcotte himself was sensitive to the pattern of religious references, in which he found a source of hope. The idealized dead father, in his loving paternalism and his creative relationship with the land, could easily be identified with God the Father, and his absence suggests a world deprived of grace, in which Isabelle-Marie nevertheless ritualistically dispenses bread and wine. Marcotte found a sign of incipient salvation in the longing that overtakes Isabelle-Marie, as she faces death, for "a God, a single God." And in the final act of Patrice, who seeks in the depth of the lake the soul he had always lacked, Marcotte saw the central quest of the work itself: "the great adventure of the recovery of the soul."

Blais's early critics focused on the novel's insistent distance from the realism that had been a mainstay of the Quebec novel. It seemed unnecessary to relate this dreamlike world of characters, who were labeled "monstrous" by the author herself,[5] to the real world of contemporary Quebec. But in 1959 these critics could hardly know that their society was on the brink of a massive process of modernization and secularization to be touched off by the election of the Liberal premier Jean Lesage in 1960. Only when the so-called Quiet Revolution was well under way could *La Belle Bête* be seen in the context of this change, a political rereading that was certainly encouraged by the evident references to current social issues in Blais's prize-winning novel of 1965, *Une saison dans la vie d'Emmanuel.*

The Belgian critic Lucien Goldmann, who saw novels as expressions of their sociohistorical context, offered his reflections on this aspect of *Une saison dans la vie d'Emmanuel* when he spoke at the University of Montreal in 1967,[6] a reflection subsequently expanded to include *La Belle Bête*. Both works, he said, revealed the contemporary conflict between young Québécois intellectuals and the traditional French-Canadian society they were attempting to change. In *La Belle Bête* the old Quebec is embodied in the mother, who, according to Goldmann, is "mortally ill and condemned to death," as signified by her facial cancer. Her admiration for the intellectually diminished Patrice reflects the attitude of Quebec's spiritual leaders, who find beauty in the culture's backwardness, for which they themselves are responsible. Isabelle-Marie attempts to rebel against the traditional society, whose mentality and values she hates, although she, like the discontented intellectuals of the time in which Blais was writing, is ultimately powerless to effect change. In Goldmann's reading, the despairing ending, with its murder and double suicide, reflects Blais's denunciation of this society, as well as her inability, in 1959, to envision a different future. Not only does Goldmann place Blais's work in its sociopolitical context, but he also makes the connection between Blais's vaguely defined rural world and the world of the traditional Quebec novel. In his view, *La Belle Bête* relied on the same structural premises of conflict between country and city as Louis Hémon's *Maria Chapdelaine* (1913), which had long served as a model for the Quebec rural novel, as well as Gabrielle Roy's more recent novel of urbanization, *Bonheur d'occasion* (1945).

The examples chosen by Goldmann are significant: not only are these two novels major examples of the Quebec rural tradition (the *roman de la terre,* or the rural novel), but they are works focused on the relationships of mothers and daughters. If both are, in some sense, allegorical representations of the plight of Quebec, the choice facing the Québécois is embodied in a daughter's decision to repeat or reject her mother's life.[7] This is the way in which Hémon frames the tragic choice of Maria Chapdelaine at the end of the novel, when, still mourning the death of her beloved François Paradis, she must choose between her two remaining suitors. If she rejects a prosperous life in the States in favor of drudgery on her neighbor's farm, it is because she is committed to reliving the model of fidelity to the land embodied in her recently dead mother. Hémon offered a famous formulation of French-Canadian ideology: "Au pays de Québec rien ne doit mourir, rien ne doit changer [In the country of Quebec nothing must die, nothing must change]."[8] This saying advocates a pattern of circular repetition appropriately embodied in his protagonist's decision to repeat her mother's life.

More than 30 years later, in *Bonheur d'occasion (The Tin Flute),* Gabrielle Roy re-creates the dilemma of Maria Chapdelaine in an urban setting in the relationship of Roseanna and Florentine Lacasse. But the attitude of Florentine is radically different from that of Maria. Although Florentine admires her mother's heroic devotion to the family, she refuses to follow the same route of pious self-sacrifice. As in *Maria Chapdelaine,* the interaction with the traditional ideology is played out in the relationship of mother and daughter, but in the 1945 novel the daughter explicitly rejects the mother's system of values, although she does not reject the mother herself. By the time Blais wrote *La Belle Bête* in 1959, however, the tension between tradition, embodied in the long-time premier Maurice Duplessis, and the forces of modernization had reached a breaking point. In this context it is not surprising that the mother and daughter of *La Belle Bête* have no possibility of communication. The mother rejects the daughter because of her "ugliness," her failure to reflect back to the mother her own self-image. In her obsession with her reflection in the mirror, the mother embodies the narcissistic complacency of Quebec's leaders, capable of accepting only those who, like her idiot son, mindlessly reenact their values. In this situation of cultural impasse the daughter's revolt must take violent form, and she sets fire to the whole traditional structure. As Margaret Atwood points out in *Survival,* her landmark study of Canadian literature, this gesture of burning down the "Ancestral Mansion" is repeated in several other Quebec works of the same era, including Blais's own *Une saison dans la vie d'Emmanuel,* where the children burn down the school.[9]

The daughter's murder of her mother represents the ultimate breakdown of a relationship that had ensured the continuity of values in the Quebec literary tradition. And the murder depicted by Blais echoes a violence against the mother appearing in other texts associated with this period of radical change. A well-known example is Anne Hébert's story "Le Torrent," where a child (in this case, a son) kills an allegorical mother figure by allowing her to be trampled by a wild horse, much as Patrice kills his stepfather in *La Belle Bête.*

It should be noted that, if Blais's allegory seems to advocate a violent break with a certain vision of the past, it does not represent a rejection of the heroic Quebec tradition of devotion to the land. This tradition is relegated to an almost mythic past, symbolized by the dead father, whose values Isabelle-Marie shares and struggles to uphold. The parent against whom she revolts has inherited the estate after seducing the father with her vain beauty: the text calls her a prostitute. The allegory thus seems to be establishing a distinction between the still-admirable history of the Quebec people and the contemporary spokesmen who purport to represent them. Blais's nuanced view of tradition will be articulated more clearly in the forceful grandmother of *Une saison dans la vie d'Emmanuel.*

The political reading of *La Belle Bête* offers a powerful explanation of a complicated and enigmatic text. Yet it does not account for the emotional force projected by Blais's strange, puppetlike characters. The text itself indicates an awareness of their lack of depth: Louise and Lanz are compared to marionettes and mechanical dolls, and Patrice, as we are informed by the narrator, has no soul. Only Isabelle-Marie has anything resembling interiority.

But it is evident that these schematic characters are working out destructive emotions hidden deep in the family structure, and it is this psychoanalytic reading that has accounted for much of the critical interest the book has received. The myths with which Blais is working—Oedipus, Electra, Narcissus—are also those privileged by Freud, and in the world Blais imagines these conflicts are allowed to run their course, unimpeded by repression and sublimation. In *La Belle Bête* the son's jealousy, embodied in the powerful libidinal horse, does actually kill the (step)father, and his utter narcissism does lead to self-destruction. The almost total fusion and mirroring that characterizes the relationship between Louise and her son may be seen as a representation of the pre-Oedipal bonding of mother and child, and Patrice is, in a sense, a child unable to survive the necessary mother-child separation.

The numerous instances of mirroring that abound in the text[10] suggest a reference to the "mirror stage" of Jacques Lacan, which marks the child's recognition of a separate sense of self. In this sense, Patrice's final plunge into the lake in search of his reflection might represent a failure in development, his inability to define himself outside of the fluid mother-child dyad.[11] But much of the mirroring in the text takes place not only through the use of conventional reflecting devices such as Patrice's lake and Louise's vanity mirror, but through the eyes of other people. As in the work of Jean-Paul Sartre, characters seek their identity in the gaze of the other. Louise is entirely a creature of her admirers: "Belle poupée, elle flottait dans les regards contemplatifs des autres, sans se douter qu'elle serait bientôt abandonnée et flétrie" ("She basked in the admiration of others like a pretty doll, never for a moment suspecting that one day she would lie battered and abandoned").[12] The extent to which these characters define themselves through others is made clear when Isabelle-Marie does, for a time, feel herself beautiful after inventing an image of a beautiful self to be reflected back by Michaël's sightless eyes.

The most destructive instances of mirroring in *La Belle Bête* take place between mother and child. Louise loves Patrice only as a reflection of her own beauty, and she rejects him when he fails to send back this self-confirming image after his disfigurement at the hands of Isabelle-Marie. Similarly, Patrice's own positive image of himself is dependent on his mother's love: when he returns home to find her dead, he is symbolically unable to recover his old image in the mirroring surface of the lake.

With Isabelle-Marie, on the other hand, the mother-child mirroring process is one of unrelieved negativity. Louise rejects her daughter because she is not a mirror in which she wants to recognize herself, and Isabelle-Marie rejects her own daughter for the same reason, because she sees in her daughter the being her mother has already rejected in herself:

Mais c'est à Isabelle-Marie que l'enfant ressemblait. Dès sa naissance, Isabelle l'avait trouvée plus monstrueuse qu'elle-même et ce visage d'enfant, affligé de la même laideur, porteur de son sang et de ses traits labourés, la révoltait. [But she looked like Isabelle-Marie. From the day of her birth Isabelle-Marie had found the baby even more hideous than herself, and the tiny face, afflicted by the same ugliness, bearing her blood and the same tortured features, repelled her.] (102; 81)

Thus the process of negative mirroring initiated by the rejecting mother is passed on from generation to generation.

As the unloving mother obsessed with the image in her mirror, Louise resembles the wicked queen of Snow White. But Isabelle-Marie, unlike the fairy-tale heroine, is not the "fairest of them all" and cannot triumph over the older woman by her superior beauty. It is rather her mother who succeeds in destroying both of them with the poisoned apple of her rejection. Thus Blais subverts the happy ending of the fairy tale. As Jennifer Waelti-Walters has shown, she also rewrites the story of Cinderella—another victim of a cruel stepmother—by creating in Michaël a Prince Charming who turns away in horror once the magical illusion of beauty has been dispelled. While the fairy-tale Cinderella moves from the ashes of the kitchen fire to the prince's palace, Blais's Cinderella ends up in the ashes of the home she has burned down. A similar process of subversion is at work in Blais's use of Beauty and the Beast (in French, *La Belle et la bête)*, from which the novel takes its title. In most versions of the tale the beast is transformed into a handsome prince through the love of a beautiful woman. In Blais's story, however, all the characters are disfigured in the end.[13]

In rewriting these fairy tales, Blais also exposes the dangers of the cult of feminine beauty on which they depend. While fairy tales construct a world in which goodness is inevitably connected to beauty, in Blais's tormented universe external appearances are irreparably severed from internal reality, expressed in Blais's repeated use of the word "soul," creating a system of distorted values that must eventually fall victim to its own contradictions. As Waelti-Walters and others have pointed out, Blais does not suggest a way out of the dilemma: Isabelle-Marie is incapable of finding a new grounding for her identity. But by her rewriting of the fairy-tale world Blais has disrupted its neat equations of goodness with physical beauty and spiritual passivity and has challenged the traditional mode of progressing toward a happy ending, if, indeed, a happy ending is possible at all.

Chapter Three

Turning Tradition on Its Head:
Une saison dans la vie d'Emmanuel

If Blais's first three novels were set in a vaguely defined world with overtones of the fantastic, the setting of *Une saison dans la vie d'Emmanuel (A Season in the Life of Emmanuel)* is unmistakably Quebec. The location is never named, but the cold and snow, the outsized family, the omnipresence of the Catholic Church, and in fact everything in the novel proclaimed it a portrait (as some said, a vicious caricature) of the old world of rural Quebec. Even as Blais was writing this novel in the mid-1960s, the Quebec of her childhood was undergoing a definitive change as a consequence of the Quiet Revolution, and the modern, secular Quebec that was emerging bore little resemblance to the world portrayed in the novel. In the virulence of her attack on the old order, Blais herself became a participant in the movement toward social change.

Like many of the Quebec novels that had preceded it, *Une saison dans la vie d'Emmanuel* is about a family, a large family. The Emmanuel of the title is the sixteenth child of parents too exhausted by work in the fields to pay attention to their swarming offspring. The parental role is filled by the indomitable grandmother, Antoinette, a larger-than-life figure who embodies the energy, patience, and tenacity that had made survival possible in this harsh northern climate. A complex and ambiguous character, Grand-Mère Antoinette confronts the reader in Blais's much-praised opening scene, where she is seen from the limited perspective of the newborn Emmanuel:

> Les pieds de Grand-Mère Antoinette dominaient la chambre. Ils étaient là, tranquilles et sournois comme deux bêtes couchées, frémissant à peine dans leurs bottines noires, toujours prêts à se lever: c'étaient des pieds meurtris par de longues années de travail aux champs (lui qui ouvrait les yeux pour la première fois dans la poussière du matin ne les voyait pas encore, il ne connaissait pas encore la blessure secrète à la jambe, sous le bas de laine, la cheville gonflée sous la prison de lacets et de cuir . . .) des pieds nobles et pieux (n'allaient-ils pas à l'église chaque matin en hiver?) des pieds vivants qui gravaient pour toujours dans la mémoire de ceux qui

les voyaient une seule fois—l'image sombre de l'autorité et de la patience. [Grand-Mère Antoinette's feet dominated the room. They lay there like two quiet, watchful animals, scarcely twitching at all inside their black boots, always ready to spring into action; two feet bruised by long years of work in the fields (opening his eyes for the first time in the dusty morning light, he couldn't see them yet, was not yet aware of the hidden wound in the leg, beneath the woolen stocking, of the ankles swollen within their prisons of leather and laces . . .), two noble and pious feet (did they not make the journey to church once every morning, even in winter?), two feet brimming with life, and etching forever in the memories of those who saw them, even only once, their somber image of authority and patience.][1]

Although Emmanuel's survival through his first winter provides a framework for the novel, it is more concerned with his adolescent brothers and sisters—the mystical and sexually obsessed Héloïse, the sleepy Pomme (Apple), the ironically named Fortuné (better known as Le Septième, Number Seven), and, most of all, the budding poet Jean Le Maigre (literally, John the Skinny). The favorite of his grandmother, who tries to protect his fragile health by putting him into a monastery, Jean Le Maigre nevertheless succumbs to tuberculosis, with the help of the diabolical Frère Théodule. He leaves his brothers to be sent off to the city, where Pomme loses three fingers in a factory accident and Number Seven embarks on a career of petty crime. Héloïse, too, leaves the farm to find sensual fulfillment and apparent happiness in a brothel.

If Jean Le Maigre is the protagonist—a conclusion suggested by Blais's insertion of his first-person autobiography in the central section of the novel—*Une saison dans la vie d'Emmanuel* tells the story of the tragic fate of the writer in this inhospitable climate. Blais began the painful process of writing this story in the winter of 1963, against the gray snow of a Massachusetts winter. In her creation of Jean Le Maigre she saw the experience of young poets condemned to die in an ignorant and oppressive world, as much in the slums of Cambridge, in which she was then living, as in the impoverished farms and factories of Quebec:

Il y a dans mon ghetto de Cambridge, des Jean-le Maigre qui cirent les chaussures des Blancs, des enfants méprisés—s'ils sont nés poètes, leurs oeuvres ne seront jamais écrites. Car ils seront drogués, ils iront en prison, ce seront peut-être des enfants criminels. [In my Cambridge ghetto there are Jean Le Maigres who shine the shoes of white people, neglected children—if they are born to be poets, their works will never be written.

Because they will be drug addicts, they will end up in prison, they may be juvenile delinquents]. (*Parcours,* 81)

She connects Jean Le Maigre to the great *poètes maudits* of history, particularly the youthful Rimbaud, whose *Une saison en enfer* is echoed in Blais's title.[2] He is also related to the great Quebec poet Emile Nelligan, who wrote his life work before being confined to an asylum at the age of 19. The poems Jean Le Maigre spews forth at every moment offer a humorous pastiche of Nelligan's melancholy: "Combien funèbre la neige / Sous le vol des oiseaux noirs" ["How funereal the snow / Beneath the black flight of the birds"] (31; 23).

Similarly, Jean Le Maigre's adolescent sexual experimentation parodies Rimbaud's famous *dérèglement de tous les sens.* Blais's novel spells out the way in which Jean Le Maigre's poetic vocation is constantly thwarted by his social milieu—by his illiterate father who opposes education, by the inadequacy of this education itself, and, finally, by the perverted world of the monastery, which offers the intellectual his only refuge. The fact that Blais herself had found it easier to write in self-imposed exile from Quebec suggests the possibility of a connection between the plight of Jean Le Maigre and her own experience, which she explores in the quasi-autobiographical *Manuscrits de Pauline Archange.* A further connection between author and character is implied by the fact that the perspective taken by Jean Le Maigre in his first-person autobiography is not far distant from that adopted by the unnamed third-person narrator of *Une saison dans la vie d'Emmanuel.* Both express their revolt against the limitations of this enclosed world by condemning it with scathing humor and transforming it with the magic of their words. As Blais's narrator has elevated to mythic stature the mundane reality of life on the farm, Jean Le Maigre transforms the story of his birth into a fairy tale of predestined greatness:

> Dès ma naissance, j'ai eu le front couronné de poux! Un poète, s'écria mon père, dans un élan de joie. Grand-Mère, un poète! Ils s'approchèrent de mon berceau et me contemplèrent en silence. Mon regard brillait déjà d'un feu sombre et tourmenté. Mes yeux jetaient partout dans la chambre des flammes de génie. [From the day I was born, I have worn a crown of lice on my head! A poet, my father cried, in a burst of joy. Grand-Mère, a poet! They approached my cradle and gazed down at me in silence. My gaze glowed already with a dark and tormented fire. My eyes sent flames of genius shooting all through the room.] (65; 52)

A portrait of the artist, *Une saison dans la vie d'Emmanuel* is at the same time a portrait of Quebec. In his introduction to the English translation, Edmund Wilson found the novel "filled with the turbid and swirling sediment of the actual French Canadian world—with that squalor and the squirming life that swarms in the steep-roofed cement-covered houses of the little Canadian towns" (vi). Even in France, where *Une saison dans la vie d'Emmanuel* was awarded the prestigious Prix Médicis, readers were sure they had discovered a work that was authentically French Canadian. Writing in *Le Figaro,* Claude Mauriac termed it a novel "written in our language that no one in France could have written."[3]

But the meaning of Blais's vision of French-Canadian life was open to interpretation. Many readers assumed Blais had painted a realistic portrait of life in rural Quebec. French critics admiringly noted her affinities with Zola, while in Quebec she drew fire for perceived inaccuracies: critics were particularly offended by her harsh treatment of the Church and her insulting portrait of the French-Canadian grandmother.

Others found that the real significance of this novel lies in its ability to move beyond the simple realistic approach taken by previous Quebec writers to create a visionary world with a density and coherence of its own. Some also began to sense that it was not a reflection of lived experience but a parodic reworking of a cultural myth. For Lucien Goldmann, *Une saison dans la vie d'Emmanuel* was not a representation of a real society but "a quasi-mythical universe born of the almost rigorous transposition of the vision of French-Canadian society and its history possessed by a large number of intellectuals" (Goldmann, 353–54). The Quebec critic Gilles Marcotte, who had been one of the first to recognize Blais's genius, pointed out that the impression of reality generated by Blais's novel was due not to its accurate representation of lived experience but, rather, its constant reference to a well-known cultural text, the *roman de la terre* and the ideology of *survivance* to which it was intimately related.[4]

Developed in the nineteenth century as a response to economic and political domination by the English, *survivance* called on Francophones to remain implanted on their farms, far from the corrupting influences of the English-speaking cities, and faithful to the teachings of the Catholic Church. In an effort to maintain Francophone voting strength, clerical spokesmen glorified the large family in a policy that became known as *la revanche des berceaux,* the revenge of the cradle. A genre that embodied this cultural ideal, the traditional Quebec rural novel was centered on a family rather than an individual protagonist and focused on the conflict between country and city life, tradition and modernization—always, of course, coming out on the side of tradition. These structures were clearly echoed in *Une saison dans la vie d'Emmanuel.*

The text of the *roman de la terre* is thus also a cultural text, and it is this text, rather than any social reality, that Blais set out to rewrite with a black humor not evident in her previous three novels. If the *roman de la terre* had shown a happy family presided over by a strong father and loving mother, Blais gives the reader a family reduced to exhausted anonymity by the sheer effort of reproduction. The numerous children are classified by numbers and letters. One of the major characters is called Number Seven, and his sisters are referred to as the big A's (Aurelia, Anita, Anna) and the little a's. Blais's narrator compares them to a herd of cows, distinguished only by size:

> Les Roberta-Anna-Anita avancèrent comme un lent troupeau de vaches, chacune entourant de ses larges bras une espiègle petite fille aux cheveux tressés, qui, dans quelques années leur ressemblerait, et qui, comme elles, soumise au labeur, rebelle à l'amour, aurait la beauté familière, la fierté obscure d'un bétail apprivoisé. [Roberta Anna Anita moved forward like a slow herd of cows, each encircling in her thick arms a lively little girl with braided hair, who in a few years would look just like them, and like them also, under the yoke of fieldwork and hostile to love, would move with the familiar beauty of cattle and their hidden pride.] (45; 35)

The mere effort of producing this brood seems to have been too much for the parents, whose absence of individual personality is signaled by their lack of a name: Blais calls them simply "the mother" and "the father" (or "the man"). Worn out by endless maternities and work in the fields, the mother is always silent and hardly has strength to nurse her latest baby. Oblivious to the many children around her, she is moved only by memories of her dead babies, who are almost as numerous, and even they soon become indistinguishable in her mind. But the system leaves little room for maternal feelings: years earlier, as the mother had mourned the death of two children in the course of a single year, the parish priest had cheerfully proclaimed the event a sign of God's love. The father's presence in the family is wholly negative: he repeatedly rapes the mother and beats his sons into submission. Hostile to education or any form of progress, he sees a life of milking cows and cutting wood as the limits of human possibility.

Only Grand-Mère Antoinette fills the void left by the anonymous parents. If the names of Grand-Mère Antoinette and her late husband, Grand-Père Napoléon, are relics of a glorious French past, their power to transmit the cultural legacy is limited by defective institutions. The grandmother's spiritual advisor is a priest unable to distinguish north from south: he literally never knows which way he is going. The school in which she places her hopes for education has an almost-illiterate schoolmistress and a dictionary that ends at the letter H, and the monastery to which she sends the gifted Jean Le Maigre is presided over by a sadistic pervert (helpfully named Théo Crapula).

An important aspect of Blais's subversion of the traditional novel is her departure from the time-honored mode of realism and omniscient third-person narration, which had dominated Quebec fiction until the 1950s. If she allows the highly individualistic first-person narrative of Jean Le Maigre to break into what is apparently a traditional narrative form, she reveals her unwillingness to abide by the accepted narrative rules. Similarly, her use of point-of-view technique in the other sections is capricious and undisciplined. Her introductory presentation of the feet of Grand-Mère Antoinette as seen from the perspective of the newborn Emmanuel is a literary tour de force, but its sophisticated analysis is hardly an accurate representation of the thoughts of a baby. And when Emmanuel is not available to act as a reflector, an unidentified narrative voice simply goes on with the story, as it does at the end of Jean Le Maigre's autobiography (since he cannot logically be expected to narrate his own death). Blais uses narrative conventions only to subvert them. Like Jean Le Maigre, she expresses both her refusal of repressive literary institutions and a new freedom to create her own narrative voice.

In her admittedly selective use of first-person narration and point of view technique Blais does manage to identify the viewpoint of her narrator and prepare a place for her reader. This is particularly true of the opening scene, where the naive perspective of the infant, who sees events and people without benefit of the usual ideological justifications, serves to establish Blais's own alienated vision of reality. The use of the newborn's perspective, unrealistic though it is, also establishes the way in which her book, perhaps the Quebec tradition itself, is to be read. The grandmother first appears as an overwhelming, potentially crushing presence, but the reader is made to share Emmanuel's realization that she is really frail and thin, and she grows progressively weaker as he grows stronger. The reader is asked to identify not with her but with the baby, whose life will clearly move beyond his grandmother's world.

Une saison dans la vie d'Emmanuel is a cruel parody of the *roman de la terre,* and many of its characters are simple caricatures. But the grandmother whose presence dominates the novel is a figure of great complexity, who reflects the writer's profound ambivalence toward the Quebec cultural past. Lucien Goldmann sees in this novel the same schema of revolt against an oppressive tradition that first appears in *La Belle Bête,* but if this is so, the maternal figure chosen to embody this oppressive past has undergone a fundamental change. Although she is weakened in the end, she is characterized by her energy and nurturant power: she is "brimming with life," as announced by the opening scene. It is never Grand-Mère Antoinette who becomes the object of the children's revolt, and, in fact, the proper relationship to her may be suggested by the impassioned dialogues in which the growing Emmanuel engages her.

Because Grand-Mère Antoinette is an ambiguous character, the nature of Blais's political vision has become an object of discussion. If, as Henri Mitterand has pointed out, Blais has failed to delineate the economic mechanisms at work in this universe,[5] it is perhaps because economics are not at the heart of her critique. Blais's focus is evident in the opening scene, where the monologue in which Grand-Mère Antoinette presents her philosophy of life is punctuated by the cries of the infant Emmanuel demanding his mother's breast. But this nourishment is denied him, as is the physical warmth he so desperately seeks from his grandmother. Refusing him contact with her body, as she has always refused "man's desire," Grand-Mère Antoinette offers him only baths in icy water, the symbolic equivalent of her austere philosophy of life. In Blais's portrayal, Grand-Mère Antoinette's most significant failing is her refusal of desire. The world Blais has created is destructive not because it has refused to adapt to modernization or set up an adequate educational system—these were problems that had already been identified by the politicians of the Quiet Revolution—but because it constantly suppresses love and desire. Blais's descriptions of Jean Le Maigre's adolescent sexual experimentation and Héloïse's sexual awakening are thus not irrelevant touches of perversion, as her critics have implied, but an integral part of her social analysis.

The constant frustration of desire is related to the persistent thematics of cold and heat. The Quebec rural novel had characteristically been structured by the rotation of the seasons, but *Une saison dans la vie d'Emmanuel* has only one season, and that is winter. Blais subverts the reassuring pattern of the natural cycle by her relentless focus on winter—a winter she herself has termed both physical and moral. As she said in an interview, "Ce que j'ai voulu faire sentir, c'est l'hiver. L'hiver moral, hiver physique, la misère matérielle et la misère morale, la prison du gel et des préjugés [What I wanted readers to feel is winter. Winter in the physical and moral sense, material and moral poverty, the prison of ice and prejudice]."[6]

The children—at least those who have the strength to resist the numbing cold of their milieu—constantly burn with desire—one that ranges from Emmanuel's yearning for his mother's breast to the more genitally oriented pleasures of Jean Le Maigre, Number Seven, and Héloïse. The need for warmth is as primary to the newborn baby as his need for his mother's milk. He yearns to fall asleep on his grandmother's breast—"on voulait dormir en elle, comme dans un fleuve chaud, reposer sur son coeur" ["you wanted to go to sleep in her, as in some warm river, to lie and rest upon her heart"] (9; 5)—but instead he is bathed in ice water and finds himself left in a cold room with icy sheets. The older children, too, constantly suffer from the cold, and their sexual experimentation is connected with their huddling together to keep warm. When Jean Le Maigre dreams of death, he sees himself falling through a hole in the ice. It is no wonder that he and Number Seven spend their time trying to set things afire (in fact, one of their first targets is the grandmother's cold sheets). The school they attend has an inadequate stove and no wood, and Number Seven's insistence that they must light a fire results in their burning down the school itself.

Grand-Mère Antoinette, conversely, is at home with the cold. If she spends her time washing her grandchildren's lice-ridden heads under the cold water of the pump, it is connected with her effort to put them all into the seminary, to enclose them all in her own celibate world. As Jean Le Maigre's creative ability seems related to his willingness to give direct expression to his desires, his voice is ultimately silenced by the lethal ministrations of the sadistic Frère Théodule, whose perversion is the consequence of an entire life spent, as Blais puts it, in "la sombre forêt des frères" ["the somber forest of the Brothers"] (107). He, too, is a victim of a celibate institution that attempts to suppress sexuality.

The character in whom sexual desire is most evident is Héloïse, who, consumed by feminine adolescent fantasies, is the only child in the family who finally realizes her dream of liberated sexuality. The brothel where she makes her career is a mirror image of the convent that Grand-Mère Antoinette had first seen as the answer to her longings—a connection that Blais makes clear in the dream of happiness that precedes Héloïse's departure from home:

> Cette fois le couvent avait été transformé en une hôtellerie joyeuse que fréquentaient des hommes gras et barbus, des jeunes gens aux joues roses,

à qui Héloïse offrait l'hospitalité et les religieuses faisaient brûler de l'encens à la cuisine pour les visiteurs. Héloïse était aimée. [This time the convent had been transformed into a joyful tavern frequented by fat, bearded men, and by young men with pink cheeks, to whom Héloïse had offered hospitality for the night. She received them in her cell. The other nuns were burning incense in the kitchen for their visitors. Héloïse was loved.] (119; 97)

The analogies between brothel and convent are in fact striking: the plump Madame Enbonpoint acts as a tender mother superior concerned with her charges, and the erotic pictures that adorn Héloïse's room remind her of Mary and the saints. Blais uses this positive image of the brothel not, certainly, to justify the practice of prostitution but to turn the traditional value system on its head. On the one hand, the convent is exposed as an institution, like the family, devoted to suppressing any real expression of human love. The connection between the religious institution and the cutting off of love and desire is made all too clear in the explicit reference to the fate of the medieval Héloïse and Abelard, castrated and condemned to celibacy as the result of their desire.

In her portrayal of Héloïse, Blais offers a detailed account of the way in which the unrecognized sexual yearnings of the adolescent girl can be manipulatively channeled into religious devotion, forever enclosing sensual women in cold convent cells. But the reversal of values cuts both ways: if religious institutions function to suppress human love, prostitution—that is, the exploitation of women's sexuality—is revealed to be at the base of the most respected social institutions. The sacrosanct large family is shown to be the result of a series of brutal rapes, which suggests that the frigidity of Grand-Mère Antoinette is perhaps not without its causes. The other jobs open to the hapless Héloïse, as described by the want ads for nurses and babysitters, are also transparent efforts to exploit women's sexuality along with their nurturant skills. Given the alternatives, the brothel represents a rational and honest choice.

If prostitution constitutes the hidden reality of recognized social institutions, the brothel itself is also an integral part of the institutional structure. Despite rhetorical condemnations from the parish priest, Madame Embonpoint is shown to be a respected citizen, and her establishment is patronized by the local elite. Indeed, in this society of repression the brothel fulfills a deep-seated need, for it is only here that the frustrated yearning for maternal affection, first seen in the infant Emmanuel, can finally be fulfilled. At the end of the novel Héloïse recognizes in the notary who has become her regular client "le gros enfant des premiers appétits, suspendu à son sein, exploitant sous toutes sortes de gestes et d'emportements . . . la soif, la grande soif du premier jour, malheureusement inassouvie" ["a big baby with primal appetites, suspended from her nipple, exploiting in all kinds of gestures and sudden transports . . . the thirst, the huge thirst of that first day, unfortunately unassuaged"] (161; 133). Near the end of the story, then, the reader is called back to the opening scene. Sexuality and the human need for affection with which it is intimately connected has gone awry in the world Blais portrays. The denial of maternal warmth leaves men to express their desire in exploitive gestures that in turn give rise to feminine frigidity. Attempts to break this cycle of denial are met with the firm resistance of the social institutions, which use sexuality for their own ends of increasing the population and supporting the authority of the Church.

The novel's closing scene is notable for its ambiguity, and it has inspired mutually contradictory interpretations. While it certainly leaves more room for optimism than the unremittingly bleak image of an abandoned orphan that had ended *La Belle Bête,* Grand-Mère Antoinette's final assertion that "all is well" is in many ways ironic. On the level of plot, Jean Le Maigre has died, Pomme has been permanently crippled, Number Seven is about to enter a life of petty crime, and Héloïse is in a brothel. The adolescent children have all been killed or maimed by their environment. But despite the outcome of the story line, hope is present in the final image of the still indomitable grandmother and the already assertive infant responding to the arrival of another spring. Named for the Messiah, Emmanuel, perhaps a new Jean Le Maigre, may somehow be able to escape the fate of his brothers and sisters. It is true that *Une saison dans la vie d'Emmanuel* offers no blueprint for the future, but the choice of a newborn baby as the source of both title and point of view indicates the extent to which this novel, unlike the preceding three, is resolutely turned toward a future perhaps open to new possibilities.

Of Blais's intended sequel to *Une saison dans la vie d'Emmanuel,* entitled *Testament de Jean-le Maigre à ses frères,* only two short sections were to see publication. The first segment, published in *Liberté* in 1972,[7] recounts the return home of a pregnant Héloïse accompanied by a prospective husband, only to be rebuffed by the still-prudish Grand-Mère Antoinette. The second segment, "La Nouvelle Institutrice," was reprinted as the opening selection in Blais's 1992 short story collection, *L'Exilé,* and it shows the direction that work might have taken. The central figure, the adolescent schoolmistress Judith Prunelle, is an androgynous Jean Le Maigre, hardly older than the adolescent poet at the time of his death but proud in her certification as a teacher and sure of the reasons for her rebellion against the old rural Quebec, in which she nevertheless finds herself enmeshed.

Clearly a child of the Quiet Revolution, which began to move control of education out of the hands of the Church, Judith rejects offers of help from the local parish priest and looks instead to the secular inspector general, who, unfortunately, has never bothered to come to this remote village. Her dialogue with the Abbé Philippe is a veritable declaration of independence from clerical control. When the priest offers to give her grammar lessons in exchange for finding students for his catechism classes, the young school teacher cuts him short:

> —Pas besoin de grammaire, dit Judith Prunelle, pas besoin de vous.
> —Les mathémathiques, peut-être?
> —J'connais mon calcul, dit Judith Prunelle, pas besoin de vous!
> [—I don't need grammar, said Judith Prunelle, no need for you.
> —Math, perhaps?
> —I know my arithmetic, said Judith Prunelle, no need for you.]
>
> (*L'Exilé,* 12)

The subjects she intends to teach in her school will be free of clerical influence and, as can be gathered from her recited lists of kings and queens of France—all Charles and Charlottes—they will be rooted in secular history. Even her story of the creation of the world, with which she begins her class, impatiently brushes aside the image of a bearded creator seated in the heavens to describe the beauty of the creation at the moment when, as in a Quebec spring, the waters begin to flow. Judith, like her biblical namesake, is a proud warrior, capable of metaphorically decapitating the leader of the opposing forces (although the weak and confused Abbé Philippe is no latter-day Holofernes). She does not hesitate to threaten him with her fists, a skill she has acquired from previous bouts with her seven brothers, from whom she has also learned to chop her own wood to heat the school. As the story recalls from *Une saison dans la vie d'Emmanuel,* it was the teacher's inability to provide adequate heating that provoked Jean Le Maigre's brothers to light the fire that burned down the school. Drawing on the strength of Quebec tradition, Judith is capable of undertaking the struggle to liberate the future grandchildren of Grand-Mère Antoinette.

But even as her personal resources are great, her material assets are meager. Her tattered suitcase is filled with carrots, a food known as an important agricultural staple of Quebec (a common, unkind rejoinder to arguments for Quebec's independence was the scenario of an independent Quebec living on milk and carrots, the only goods it was supposedly capable of producing). While the carrots are enough for her own needs, they are clearly inadequate to feed the family of starving children with whom she is immediately confronted, and she castigates the priest for failing to provide her with needed bread. Similarly, the children's mother, driven mad by her life with an alcoholic father, wanders the country roads begging alms for the poor from the silent trees and the peaceful but unresponsive heavens. Judith Prunelle may be intrepid, but the problems she confronts are severe. Although the proud figure of their neighbor, Grand-Mère Antoinette, is mentioned, the children in Judith's class are deprived of all parental support. Their mother is mad, their father sick, and their alcoholic grandfather threatens to shoot them in his drunken rages. Chester, the youngest of the children, clearly suffers from mental retardation, a situation to which the grandfather responds, as to the mother's madness, by saying it's all in the family. Seen as an inescapable factor of their own nature—perhaps even deserved because inherited—the grandfather's wisdom, like the resignation to God's will embodied in the traditional Quebec culture, leaves no room for progress toward change.

The oldest of the children, Joséphine Poitiers, herself has the energy to protect the others and to turn her aspirations into words. But her stories, as in some rural Catholic communities, seek hope in visions of the Virgin Mary, who nevertheless seems strangely powerless to help. In one pathetic vision the Virgin asks Joséphine to boil milk for her baby, but the girl is able to find no milk in her kitchen, even though she lives on a farm. As the words that flow from Joséphine's active imagination struggle with Judith's stories for control of the class, the battle is engaged. Although it was never completed, giving way before the demands of Blais's own story in the three-volume *Manuscrits de Pauline Archange,* the tale of the strong young girls in *Testament de Jean-le Maigre à ses frères* may well have gone in a different direction from that of Jean Le Maigre and his brothers.

Chapter Four

Adolescents in Revolt: *Tête Blanche, David Sterne,* and *Pierre*

"Tête Blanche," as the blonde protagonist of Blais's second novel is nicknamed by his mother, is one of a long line of troubled adolescents who form the center of much of Blais's fiction, most notably Jean Le Maigre of *Une saison dans la vie d'Emmanuel* and Anna of *Visions d'Anna.* The affinity shown by many of these adolescents to the semiautobiographical Pauline Archange, whose apparent hard-heartedness is transparently an effort to protect her sensitivity against the suffering of the world around her, suggests that this type of character may bear a special relationship to the author's own experience. Like Tête Blanche, the title characters of the novels *David Sterne* and *Pierre* provide a violent acting out of the responses of sensitive adolescents to a cruel and meaningless world.

Tête Blanche

Much like Isabelle-Marie of *La Belle Bête,* published a year earlier, Tête Blanche is a solitary child torn by impulses to cruelty and tenderness. Unlike Isabelle-Marie, however, he is not a one-dimensional figure engaged in living out a mythic plot: the adolescent Evans inhabits a world much like our own, although the physical and social background for the handful of characters in the novel is only vaguely sketched in. But the abandonment felt by Tête Blanche after the divorce of his parents and the subsequent death of his mother is more easily recognizable as part of our daily experience than the fairy-tale adventures of Isabelle-Marie.

In the loneliness of this boarding-school student who idealizes a distant mother, Philip Stratford has seen a parallel with François Mauriac's novel *La Pharisienne,* although Blais's epistolary narrative lacks the rich social tapestry that characterizes Mauriac's novelistic universe. Judging from the reading available to the characters of Blais's autobiographical *Manuscrits de Pauline Archange,* Mauriac was a staple of Quebec bookstores in the 1950s. Given the large role played by Catholicism in pre–Quiet Revolution Quebec life, it is not surprising that a vocabulary with overtones of Mauriac, of isolation from God, and the threat of damnation is part of the texture of Blais's novel.

While it is often a subject of commentary, the problem of grace and salvation never becomes a central concern in the novel. The salvation sought by Tête Blanche lies in human contact rather than divine, in the love of his lost mother briefly reborn in his romantic friendship with the maternal Emilie. There are intense discussions of the individual's relationship to God in the exchange of letters between the isolated and skeptical Tête Blanche and Emilie, who retains a serene faith in God despite the attacks of her frivolous mother and atheistic father. The dominant theme, however, is a psychological one, although it is couched in religious terms. Blais seems to profess a profoundly Manichean view of human beings torn between the forces of good and evil, although the evil most feared by Tête Blanche is within himself. As he writes to Emilie, "Au fond, tous les êtres humains sont comme moi. Ils portent le désir du mal et le désir du bien. En moi, le désir du mal est le plus fort. Je le sais" ["On the whole, all human beings are the same as I am. They have in them a desire to do evil and a desire to do good. In me, the desire for evil is the stronger. I know that"].[1] This vision of human beings, particularly adolescents, as the battleground of conflicting desires continues to be an important element in Blais's vision of the world, although in later works its explicit religious overtones tend to disappear.

This spiritual view of the world became a subject of controversy at the moment of the book's appearance, perhaps spurred by the praise of the Toronto journalist and critic Scott Symons, who had met Blais while taking a course at Laval University. Symons admired Blais's acknowledgment of the existence of evil—a concept that, in his view, the modern world would like to deny. Symons saw Blais's novel as a refusal of what he termed "Americanization," an attitude based on the suppression of Original Sin, and he went on to identify this aspect of Blais's vision with the "mission" of a French-Canadian culture shipwrecked in a sea of North American Protestants who had long ago lost touch with their soul.[2] The Quebec critic André Belleau, on the other hand, found in the world constructed by Blais outdated remnants of German romanticism, seeing in her murky settings "a Walt Disney version of a German town of the romantic era." For Belleau, *Tête Blanche* is nothing more than a personal fairy tale that "deliberately situates itself outside of time, outside of *our* time."[3] For Belleau, as for Jacques Godbout and the other young secularly oriented intellectuals connected with the periodical

Liberté, the echoes of the past were more evident in Blais's work than the spirit of revolt against an oppressive world with which they would later identify in *Une saison dans la vie d'Emmanuel.*

The world of Evans's boarding school is not a Manichean universe of good and evil forces. His own acts of sporadic cruelty offer the only evidence of brutality in a school that seems to be a refuge for the hopeless of the earth. The fragile Pierre, whom Tête Blanche inexplicably shoves down the stairs in the book's opening scene, is in fact dying of tuberculosis, and his constant coughing and progressive debilitation help open Tête Blanche's eyes to what is happening to his own mother, although her short, impersonal letters try to hide the signs of her illness. Tête Blanche develops compassion for Pierre through his identification with his mother, but he continues to torment the apparently retarded Feldérik, inciting him to acts of petty destruction. At one point, he succeeds in provoking Feldérik to wantonly destroy the carefully arranged glassware of the professor who has generously invited this band of misfits to dinner.

While in some cases the boarding school serves as a hospice and home for the physically and mentally incapacitated, it also seems to double as an orphanage, receiving students like Berthil when his stepmother no longer wants to keep him after his father's death. Each boarding student has his own painful secret: Luc's father is in prison, Claude's mother manifestly prefers the company of his sisters. The solitary headmaster, the kindly Monsieur Brenner, betrays the symptoms of existential anguish as he buries himself in his Bible on Sundays and spends his free hours alone tending his pine trees. Even the beautiful and apparently carefree Emilie, with whom Tête Blanche spends a summer vacation, has been separated from her beloved father and forced to become a mother not only to her younger siblings but to her own irresponsible mother as well, who interrupts the vacation with the news of yet another unwanted pregnancy.

While the problems of Tête Blanche are not unlike those of Isabelle-Marie, another adolescent driven to violence by parental abandonment and rejection, the drama here is seldom acted out. The struggle within the characters, and especially their groping attempts to establish and maintain relationships, is shown in a variety of narrative forms that privilege their inner life. A particularly important form is epistolary—Tête Blanche's correspondence with his dying mother, with Emilie, and with his former schoolmaster. In the first segment of the book Tête Blanche shows a range of emotional development. It begins by setting the child's sense of abandonment against the seeming insensitivity of the mother's responses but moves toward the boy's recognition of his mother's illness and her growing ability to write openly and realistically. The diary form that follows provides a continuation of Tête Blanche's dialogue with his dead mother until it is replaced by his correspondence with Emilie. The brief, final section records a few letters exchanged between an older Tête Blanche, now on his own in the world, and Monsieur Brenner, his only remaining emotional tie. In the book's closing scene, Tête Blanche, teetering on the brink of adulthood, sees a figure who resembles Emilie being swept away from him in the crowd—a scene that reenacts the emotional abandonment that has always been his lot.

David Sterne

While solitary and tormented adolescents continue to appear in Blais's novels, proliferating into an entire family in *Une saison dans la vie d'Emmanuel, David Sterne,* published in 1967, is the first of her narratives to focus on a young male irresistibly drawn to destructive acts. The figure of David Sterne surges up in the midst of Blais's efforts to write a continuation of her enormously successful satire of Quebec rural life. Moving away from the specificity of the Quebec setting, Blais places her troubled adolescents in a vaguely sketched city, but, unlike the settings of *Tête Blanche,* this world is fully a product of our own time. Indeed, as signaled by the figure of the student who sets himself on fire in protest against the agents of nuclear war, this novel has been deeply affected by the particular climate in which Blais was writing. A similar death by self-immolation of a French student of the 1960s is recorded in her Wellfleet notebooks. Drawn into the atmosphere of the antiwar protests led by her friend Barbara Deming, Blais could not help but react to the accounts of military violence that saturated the media, some of which she mentions in her notebooks.

As Blais explains in her memoirs, in *David Sterne* she is telling the story of an entire generation of young people, "une génération vouée par les guerres, la guerre du Viêt-nam, la ségrégation qui a déjà fait tant de victimes, à une disparition précoce, une usure prématurée [a generation doomed by war, the Vietnam war, segregation, which has already claimed so many victims, to an early disappearance, a premature old age]" (*Parcours,* 116). The characters are based on two friends from her Cambridge years, Jack and Robert:

J'écris un roman que m'ont inspiré mes amis Jack et Robert à Cambridge,
c'est un court roman sur la responsabilité sociale, le désarroi personnel,
c'est la naissance pour moi de cet être qui m'était inconnu avant la ren-
contre de Jack, mon ami étudiant de Cambridge qui sera détruit par les
drogues, de Robert, le jeune écrivain noir meurtri à jamais par la cruauté
du racisme, ces années-là aux Etats-Unis, c'est la naissance de David
Sterne. Mes amis revivent à travers ce héros de roman qui est un personnage dont la jeunesse a été brisée. [I am writing a novel inspired by my
friends Jack and Robert from Cambridge; it is a short novel about social
responsibility, personal disintegration; it is the birth of this being who
was unknown to me before I met Jack, my student friend from
Cambridge who would be destroyed by drugs, Robert, the young black
writer forever scarred by the cruelty of racism. Those years in the United
States see the birth of David Sterne. My friends live again through this
novelistic hero whose youth has been destroyed.] (*Parcours,* 114)

Jack is a figure who has appeared from the beginning of her memoirs,
a student with whom she walks by the river in Cambridge, a draft
dodger without means of subsistence who becomes more and more
dependent on the hallucenogenic drugs popular in that era, finally a
young suicide victim. The leap from the church steeple of Michel
Rameau in the novel is Jack's plunge from the tenth story of a Boston
hotel. He leaves a mother who will forever live with his memory, alone in
their Cape Cod home, and a note that says, simply, "Je m'envole, c'est
trop dur et personne ne veut m'aider dans ma réhabilitation, je ne vois
pas non plus quand finira la guerre. Adieu [I'm taking off, it's too hard
and no one is willing to help me in my rehabilitation, and I don't see
when the war will get over. Good-bye forever]" (*Parcours,* 117). The
hatred expressed by David Sterne, on the other hand, and his relentless
persecution by the police, mirrors the feelings of Robert, the young black
writer whose persecution by white society makes him destructive to others, as he has abandoned a woman companion to a lonely death from
cancer and led his young wife to suicide. Unlike David Sterne, however,
Robert is able to find some meaning in his writing and perhaps, as he
later indicated to Blais, some atonement with his dead.

The form of the novel—broken into fragments, shifting voices and
points of view, hovering between prose and poetry—is also influenced by
the milieu in which Blais lives, but in a very specific way. Escaping from
the summer tourist invasion of Cape Cod to the quiet isolation of the
artists' colony at Skowhegan, Maine, she watches John Cage create his

music from a diversity of clashing sounds, which, in its postmodern cacophony, seems to mirror the lives of her protagonists:

> Pendant ce concert de John Cage, la forme de mon roman me préoccupe, j'aimerais entendre la voix du texte, sans doute serait-ce une voix cassée, comme la musique de John Cage; la forme n'en sera pas conventionnelle, car lorsque je pense à Jack, à Robert, aux bouleversements de ces deux existences, je me sens tressaillir des secousses, de l'énorme vertige d'être qui les ont habités tous les deux. [During that John Cage concert, I'm thinking about the form of my novel; I would like to hear the voice of the text; it would probably be a broken voice, like the music of John Cage; the form will not be conventional, because when I think of Jack and Robert, of the upheavals of these two lives, I feel myself tremble with the shocks, with the vertiginous mode of being that inhabited both of them.] (*Parcours*, 117)

Although the violence in the novel is never tied to a specific nation or conflict, the threat of war and nuclear destruction hangs over the events of the novel and provides the deeper motivation for the three adolescents whose self-inflicted deaths it describes. David Sterne, whose figure dominates the story, appears at first to be a contentious adolescent who rebels against constraints in an effort to assert his own force, to become, as he says, master of his own destiny. But his story is told in first-person narrative, and his proud assertions of destructive will slowly reveal more complicated aspects of his being. As he admits, the image presented by his interior monologue is a constantly changing adolescent self-construction: "Je sens les différentes peaux du mensonge qui se séparent de moi, non pour reconstituer un portrait véridique de moi-même, mais un modèle trompeur ambigu quelque peu à ma ressemblance qui sait? [I feel the different layers of lies that peel themselves off, not to reconstruct an accurate portrait of myself, but an ambiguous misleading model something of a likeness who knows]."[4] He presents himself as a Gidean rebel: "Je désirais soudain aller plus loin vers un sommet de gloire personnelle ma vérité je la voyais c'était la verte nuit de ma colère de mon orgueil inguérissable [I suddenly wanted to go farther toward a summit of glory I saw my truth it was the green night of my anger of my incurable pride]" (15). Like the prodigal son Gide describes, he expresses contempt for the self-satisfied life of his respectable bourgeois family and seeks the experience of hunger and cold to which a mysterious voice has invited him. But, although he experiences a similar intoxication, unlike Gide's heroes he finds no pleasure in the debauchery in which he indulges. Even the drugs that exalt his friend Michel Rameau have no effect on him. Rather, he experiences an intensification of suffering.

The philosophy he imparts to others and by which David Sterne seeks to live is expressed by his counsel to François Reine: "Allez donc jusqu'au bout de vous-même [Go to the limits of yourself]" (88). In the case of David Sterne, this reality reveals itself to be not one of Nietzschean will to domination but rather one of suffering. His crimes against himself and others—his thefts, rapes, and prostitution—seem meant to trouble the facade of unquestioning acceptance of the prevailing world order. This order, he feels, only serves to mask an underlying impulse to destruction. He comes to see the material comfort in which he has been immersed since childhood as the source of murderous wars, and he becomes a thief in order to awaken others to the evils of private property. And it is this tranquil, bourgeois security that is preserved at the cost of an arsenal of nuclear armaments: "Et puis, il n'y a pas que Dieu qui vous protège, mais cette armée, cette voûte la clôture politique qui empêche la destruction la mort de venir par surprise ces voûtes ces corridors ces murs d'armes de bombes miraculeuses toutes prêtes [And then, you not only have God protecting you but this army, the overarching vault the political wall that prevents destruction death from entering by surprise these vaults, these corridors these walls of miraculous bombs ready to go]" (36).

It is his sensitivity to the reality of suffering and destruction in the modern world that provides the link between the delinquent David and his friends Michel Rameau and François Reine, each of whom follows his own path to self-destruction. The biblical and religious resonance of their names suggests the different paths each has elected to pursue to the end. David evokes both the adolescent strength of the battle with Goliath and the debauchery of the aging King David. François suggests the gentle saintliness and concern for every living creature embodied in Saint Francis of Assisi. Michel, who kills himself by jumping from a tower, repeats the broken flight of a fallen archangel.

Michel Rameau, who shares David's boarding school, also shares his condemnation of the order of the world. Embracing as his own all humanity's crimes, Michel cannot bring himself to subscribe to the facade of innocence adopted by those around him: "'Ma culpabilité est historique,' disait-il souvent à David, 'il n'y a pas un seul crime commis sur terre dont je puisse me libérer, ni dans le présent ni dans l'avenir car je sais que mon histoire c'est l'histoire d'un massacre permanent. Voilà pourquoi je refuse l'innocence que l'on m'impose' ['My guilt is historical,' he often said to David, 'there is not a single crime committed on earth from which I can free myself, in the present or in the future for I know that my history is the history of a permanent massacre. That's why I refuse the innocence they try to impose on me']" (64–65). In this situation Michel is not free to seek his own happiness; as he says, "Quel monstrueux acte d'oubli, d'égoïsme que d'être heureux. . . . On arrache son bonheur des entrailles des autres, à chaque fois, on renouvelle le massacre des Juifs, on dévaste Hiroshima [What a monstrous act of forgetfulness, of egoism it is to be happy. You tear your happiness out of the guts of others, each time, you renew the massacre of the Jews, you devastate Hiroshima]" (70).

While David makes himself an ally of this egoistic, destructive world in order to make its nature apparent to others, Michel aspires to the peace of a remembered seaside scene: "Un paysage, oui, familier, pourtant, une grève recouverte de neige, la mer glacée (mais étrangement silencieuse), un ciel nu, sans oiseaux. En fermant les yeux, il pouvait descendre jusqu'à cette parfaite quiétude, y marcher, y vivre quelques heures [A landscape, yes, familiar, a beach covered with snow, the frozen sea (but strangely silent), an empty sky, with no birds. By closing his eyes he could descend to this perfect tranquillity, walk there, live there a few hours]" (65). But he finds this peace accessible only in death, as death offers the only way to avoid complicity with the "reign of terror" that surrounds him: "Il n'y avait plus d'espoir: tuer ou mourir [There was no hope left: kill or die]" (76).

François Reine, the law student who befriends David Sterne at his most destitute moment, is a Christ-like figure who aspires to change the order of the world, to ease the suffering of those around him. He, too, is unable to seek a separate peace in individual happiness. But as he slowly loses faith in the efficacy of his efforts to aid the poor, he comes to share David's conviction that compromise is impossible: "il faut que je connaisse une souffrance irrévocable—la paix la paix [I must experience an irrevocable suffering—peace peace]" (53). It is with these sentiments that he goes off to immolate himself in protest against the agents of war.

Joined in their uncompromising rejection of the modern world, the three adolescents are isolated from each other by an impenetrable solitude that proves stronger than their brief moments of communion, which might have provided an alternative to death. Each has walled himself off from the world of women—mother, fiancée, or sympathetic companion like the pitying Julie Brel, to whose trust David and Michel respond with a brutal rape. Maternal love is an important source of human contact in many of Blais's novels. The memory of his mother and the concern of Emilie in *Tête Blanche* provide some comfort to the child, and the strength of maternal love offers a refuge to female adolescents in *Visions d'Anna. David Sterne,* however, depicts a world of masculine isolation. Michel turns to David before undertaking his fatal jump, but he is met by a wall of silence: "si simplement David avait dit, 'Michel, il faut descendre' [If only David had said, 'Michel, you must come down']" (94). And David himself feels his desire for suffering waning as he talks with François Reine, but he asks only to be left alone as François goes off to his death. He can only dream of a potential reconciliation with Michel Rameau, in shared tenderness with Julie Brel. In the dream sequence that ends the book, David is reunited with François in a luminous seaside setting that recalls the earlier dream of Michel, until both are swept away by invading armies.

While the lonely world of Tête Blanche held the possibility of ephemeral epistolary dialogues, the story of the three solitary young men is told through a series of first-person narratives, which alternate with third-person interior monologues. Although the separate characters live through the same events and even share similar perspectives, the various voices rarely intersect: dialogues are brief and fail to provide communication. The voices of the three adolescents dominate the narrative, but Blais opens the novel to a variety of other voices—people whose lives have been touched by the three adolescents and, because of their deaths, have begun to question their own lives. David's mother, teachers of David and Michel, the poor family visited by François Reine, and even the victimized Julie Brel respond to the protagonists' concerns. This expanding multivoiced narrative looks ahead to the far-ranging narrative consciousness of *Le Sourd dans la ville* and provides a note of hope otherwise lacking to the novel by suggesting that the young men's protest may not have been totally without effect on others.

Pierre

Pierre, the protagonist of Blais's 1982 novel, could be an even more desperate younger brother to the Anna of *Visions d'Anna* or a later incarnation of David Sterne, acting out in a different mode an adolescent response to a world headed for destruction. Seeing the prevalence of violence around him, he leaves his pacifist family to join a motorcycle gang who engage in antisocial acts. While David Sterne and his friends had seemed bent on self-destruction, Pierre claims to be acting in an effort to survive, to become, as he says, "a man of my time."

The violence of the Vietnam War era had been reflected in a diffuse way in *David Sterne*, but the sources of destruction are precisely labeled in *Pierre*. The interior monologue is a collage of actual media headlines of 1981, as indicated by the original title, *Pierre, ou la guerre du printemps 1981*. Blais had spent a year collecting her material from magazines and newspapers, particularly from television. She soon found herself, like her protagonist, overwhelmed by the violence of her era: "Avec tous ces documents, on a comme l'impression d'avoir les dossiers de l'humanité entre les mains et qu'ils sont tous très laids [With all these documents, it's like having the files on all of humanity in your hands, and they are all very ugly]."[5] The effect of her collected evidence was to convince the author that contemporary humanity lives in a state of perpetual war, a feeling produced not only by the continuing fear of nuclear destruction but also by the progressive poisoning of the environment, the anti-immigrant racism of "skinheads" and other right-wing groups, destructive forms of religious fundamentalism, as evidenced in Jonestown and Iran, and increasing antisocial violence by gangs of urban youth.

Specific episodes in the novel reproduce real news headlines carefully recorded by Blais. Lurking in the background, the mythical "Great Brain" who coordinates the forces of destruction takes the media form of an ageless but still virile old man who speaks lovingly of his ranch and horses—a portrait that bears an uncanny resemblance to the former movie star who had taken office in 1981 as president of the United States. The violent voices of the media invade Pierre's interior monologues to become its very substance, producing a multivoiced narrative, not unlike that of the roving omniscient consciousness that had dominated *Le Sourd dans la ville* and *Visions d'Anna*. This narrative strategy blurs the boundaries between reality and fiction, shifting the focus from the inner reality of the characters to concrete evidence of the threatened global destruction that forms the background of Blais's other fiction of the early 1980s. It was this shift from interior to exterior that constituted Blais narrative project for this novel. As she explains, "Au temps de Balzac, on pouvait aller jusqu'au fond des personnages, étudier les êtres, c'était merveilleux. Mais aujourd'hui on est obligé de mettre la société dans laquelle vivent ces êtres. . . . La réalité, c'est ça, je ne peux pas m'en évader [In Balzac's time you could get to the bottom of characters, study human beings, it was marvelous. But today you have to show the society in which these beings live. . . . That's reality, I can't escape it]" (*Le Devoir,* 21).

The voices of the media, particularly television, form the text of this novel, as they have formed the consciousness of Pierre, Blais's 16-year-old protagonist, and have shaped his society. Despite his father's strict prohibition of war games and toys, television images have made their way into Pierre's home, bringing with them evidence of the violence of the world. The media transmit not only the words of political leaders but, more deeply penetrating the consciousness of the spectators, the images that constitute human reality. Foremost among these are the images of advertising, which are particularly important in forming our concepts of masculinity and femininity. As a standard of masculinity, the gentle pacifism of Pierre's father is clearly no match for the "Marlboro Man" warrior image that Pierre sees around him, toward which he begins to direct his aspirations:

> L'empreinte du guerrier triomphait partout. Même dans ces régions les plus reculées de la terre, l'homme surgit soudain, plaît et terrorise, parfois sous un air de banalité sans malice. Lorsqu'il propose une marque de cigarettes dans un message télévisé, avec la cigarette qui semble se dégager, compacte, du vert paquet vers le ciel, c'est lui, toujours lui qui est présent, c'est lui, muni de sa cigarette, qui rappelle à ceux qui l'oublient qu'il est le créateur d'obus, d'engins nucléaires: la cigarette n'est que sa douceur permise, atténuant un peu sa méchanceté, et je pensais, regarde, Pierre, les Alpes sont là, derrière l'homme qui fume avec insouciance. Il enveloppe la majesté des montagnes et, lorsqu'il le faut, le silence du désert. [The mark of the warrior was dominant everywhere. Even in the most remote regions of the earth, the man suddenly appears, seduces and terrorizes, sometimes with an apparent well-intentioned banality. When he promotes a brand of cigarettes in a television commercial, with the cigarette that seems to stand out against the pack, pointing toward the sky, he is always the one who is present, he is the one who, armed with his cigarette, recalls to those who have forgotten that he is the creator of shells, of nuclear weapons: the cigarette is only the relaxation he allows himself, somewhat softening his hardheartedness, and I thought, look, Pierre, the Alps are there, behind the man who is nonchalantly smoking. He encompasses the majesty of the mountains and, when necessary, the silence of the desert.][6]

The connection of a destructive virility with the toxic smoke of cigarettes links the dangers of war to the more insidious threat of environmental pollution: "j'étais viril, comme lui, je fumais amplement dans l'air du soir, cet air qui était le mien et que je pouvais enfumer de toute la toxicité de mes vices, de mes plaisirs, de mes inventions meurtrières [I was virile, like him, I smoked freely in the evening air, this air that was mine and that I could pollute with all the toxicity of my vices, my pleasures, my murderous inventions]" (13).

In *Visions d'Anna*, which Blais had published a year earlier, the feminine network of mothers and daughters offered refuge and sustenance for female adolescents in revolt against the same destructive world that confronts Pierre. But, as a young male, Pierre feels compelled to reject his family's world of feminine values in order to become a man. In the opening words of his interior monologue, he defines the rejection of femininity and the warmth and softness with which it is connected in his mind as an essential part of his project and a defining element of his symbolically appropriate name: "Je délaissais cet univers transparent, féminin, de l'amour, pour entrer dans l'âme de l'homme où ce mot 'âme' n'existait plus. Je devenais un soldat, un dieu, parmi d'autres, connaissant le pouvoir de sa force, le délire des armes. Je devenais Pierre [I abandoned the transparent feminine universe of love to enter into the soul of man where the word 'soul' no longer existed, I became a soldier, a god, among others, feeling the power of his strength, the intoxication of battle. I became Pierre]" (9–10).

Blais's understanding of Pierre unconsciously shares the outlook of much contemporary gender theory, in which masculinity can only define itself in opposition to the feminine. Nancy Chodorow, for example, argues that the protracted absence of the father from the lives of contemporary American children, combined with the omnipresence of the mother, leaves male children to define masculinity by its absence rather than identifying with positive male role models.[7] Thus Pierre sees what he thinks is an essential masculinity in the senseless brutality of his young friend Gregg as he lashes out at his own sister: "L'agressivité de Gregg éveillait en moi d'ancestrales clameurs sauvages, j'étais Gregg, la violence était la seule réalité, le fondement de ma vie [Gregg's aggression awoke in me savage ancestral clamors, I was Gregg, violence was the only reality, the foundation of my life]" (12).

As the model of solitary masculinity shapes the aspirations of Pierre, the media provide an even more debasing model for his female counterpart. She adopts the parallel name Stone, translating the characteristics of hardness and invulnerability sought by Pierre into another language and gender. While Pierre can aspire to share in the destructive force of the solitary male, Stone can only hope to become the passive object of his desires: "L'objet même, le plus dégradé, le plus humilié de tous [Nothing but an object, the most degraded, the most humiliated of all]" (40). As he watches Stone use her phallic lipstick to turn her lips into a sensual object of male desire, in imitation of the icy and artificial images of femininity distributed by the media, Pierre realizes the extent to which Stone and her media models have become "l'objet façonné par l'homme, sa possession tant de fois polie, métamorphosée, pour des raisons publicitaires, ces lèvres dont il était l'inventeur [an object shaped by man, his possession polished and repolished, reshaped for advertising purposes, these lips invented by him]" (47).

The combination of brutal, rapacious sexuality and senseless violence that constitutes his image of modern man is epitomized for Pierre in the world of motorcycle gangs, based on the Hell's Angels he had first glimpsed as a child in California. Their bodies sheathed in leather, protected from the penetrating gaze of the other by mirrored sunglasses, the bikers constantly aspire to emulate the Marlboro Man image of unfeeling and unrestrained force. Pierre's life with the motorcycle gang dominates the narrative, and the rapes and violent robberies they commit are described in graphic detail. Blais suggests, however, that they are only a younger and more visible imitation of a more powerful hidden force that controls the destinies of the world, that of the rich men sheltered in their walled estates:

Ces hommes d'affaires qui buvaient leurs cocktails, et dont le corps était aseptisé sous leur cravate à rayures ou à pois, partageaient avec notre guérilla les mythes, les structures que nous imitions à l'intérieur de leur société: dans nos rassemblements, dans nos clubs de motocyclistes, nous avions, comme dans leurs institutions bancaires, un président, un vice-président, un trésorier, des secrétaires; nous avions la force avec nous, l'énergie accumulatrice. [Those businessman who were drinking their cocktails, with their antiseptic bodies beneath their striped or polka-dot ties, shared with our guerrilla band the myths, the structures that we were imitating in their own society: in our gatherings, in our motorcycle clubs, we had, as in their banking institutions, a president, a vice-president, a treasurer, secretaries; we had strength on our side, acquisitive energy.] (35)

While Blais's attempts to point beyond this gang violence to a conspiracy directed by the "Great Brain" and his cohorts of rich financiers is not fully developed, she does focus attention on the increasing violence in the contemporary world. Unlike *Visions d'Anna,* however, *Pierre* offers the reader little in the way of a hopeful solution. Pierre, in the end, remains at a distance from the world of violence in which he has tried to immerse himself, but, in contrast to Anna, he has no plans to return home.

Chapter Five

The Fatality of the Couple:
Le Jour est noir, Les Voyageurs sacrés, L'Insoumise, and *Le Loup*

As is clear in the families she portrays in *La Belle Bête* and *Une saison dans la vie d'Emmanuel,* Blais does not see human relationships as sources of warmth and comfort. If even the love between parents and children becomes destructive in Blais's fictional universe, the same is true of romantic and sexual love between man and woman or, as in *Le Loup,* between man and man. In each of the four short novels in which Blais explores the intimacy of the couple, she shows the forces that bring them together are the same as those that ultimately tear them apart. Human beings appear powerless to create enduring relationships in the face of ever-changing passions, as in *Les Voyageurs sacrés* and *Le Loup,* and perhaps most deeply, in the face of the isolation of the individual that seems to be at the heart of the human condition, as envisioned in all these works of the 1960s and early 1970s.

It is not that the human relationships in these works happen not to work out: they are doomed from the start by a sort of fatality that seems impossible to overcome. At least Blais's work at this time can offer no solution. It is this inexorable failure of human love in a world where the yearning for human contact is a primary force that accounts for much of the darkness of Blais's vision in this period. It is only in her work of the late 1970s and beyond, beginning with *Les Nuits de l'Underground,* that she will begin to envision the possibility of relationships based on mutual caring.

Le Jour est noir

With her third novel, *Le Jour est noir,* Blais moves from the world of childhood and adolescence to the tragic dramas of adult life, particularly what she will later come to call "the fatality of the couple." As one critic has commented, the book is set somewhere "between dream and reality."[1]

Concentrating her attention, as in *La Belle Bête,* on the primary matter of human emotions, Blais keeps external details to a minimum and focuses on the inner anguish of the characters. Even an allegorical reading could suggest no relationship to the problems of Quebec, and, indeed, the novel was written during the year Blais spent in France on a Canada Council grant. But neither is the setting recognizably French. The atmosphere of fog, dark streets and empty houses is grounded not in geography but in emotion. The somber tone is lightened only by a vision of children gathering cherries at day's end—a scene whose innocent pleasure immediately gives way to the dark realities of the ensuing tale.

More a poetic narrative than a full-fledged novel, *Le Jour est noir* states and develops the theme of the solitude of the individual, in which all Blais's characters are entrapped, even as they attempt to reach out to one another in tenderness, in desire or maternal love. Each of these gestures, although it may bring momentary happiness, inevitably ends in solitude and pain for self and the other. In *Le Jour est noir* the same tragic pattern repeats itself in successive generations. The desire for isolation and self-destruction, which has led to Josué's abandonment of his family, is reborn in his daughter Roxane and leads her husband to suicide. For Blais, such situations seem rooted in the human condition.

The sources of the characters' anguish are unclear, although at several points Blais suggests a vision of universal destruction that reaches beyond the limited world of the characters. When Yance announces her pregnancy to her brother Raphaël, he replies by evoking a doomed universe:

> Yance, quelle idée de mettre un enfant au monde! Tu es donc sûre de ce monde? Il y aura un désastre. Pour nous, il ne reste que le moment aveugle, les amours aveugles, les plaisirs inconscients. Nous avons installé notre avenir dans un tout petit instant tourmenté. Nous sommes la génération de la mort. [Yance, what an idea, to bring a child into the world! Have you any faith in this world? There's going to be a disaster. For us, there is nothing left but the blind present, blind loves, thoughtless pleasures. We have set up our future in one tiny, tormented moment of time. We are the generation of death.][2]

The family of Yance and Raphaël is doomed by an inexplicable heredity to live with death: their father has committed suicide and their little brother Nicolas finally loses his long battle with an unnamed illness. Their gestures of love, even if heroic, are inevitably defeated by the realities of life and death. Geneviève, the older sister of Yance and Raphaël, devotes her life in vain to curing the doomed Nicolas. Yance abandons their child to devote herself to her husband, Josué, but she can never fulfill his undefined aspirations. And a generation later, Jessy commits suicide when he sees the same dreamy insatiability in Josué's daughter Roxane.

Although the two couples who appear in the opening scene are followed throughout the narrative, Blais's efforts to create the appearance of continuity, development, or even narrative closure seem alien to the material. *Le Jour est noir* is not a novel but a series of intense emotional encounters involving a character and a landscape. Except for the initial scene in which the four children begin the process of entering into the world of adult desire, the emotional content of each of these scenes is a variation on the theme of despair. Yance, torn between the promise of her unborn child and the knowledge that Josué is slowly slipping away from her, lives out her drama in the dark of night or on the beach on the appropriately named Ile Noire. When the same constellation of emotions is relived by Roxane, she and her husband seek refuge in a snowy wilderness.

The opening scene sets the mood of the entire narrative. Poised at the moment when a perfect summer's day passes into night, the scene of children gathering cherries marks the moment of passage from the innocent magic of childhood to a world of adulthood marked by desire and death. Yance and Raphaël, the sister and brother whose lives have already been darkened by the suicide of their father, encounter the beings who will bring tragedy into their own lives, as the symbolic acts of the summer idyll will leave indelible traces on their lives. In the unsynchronized movements of the children's swings appears the pattern that will tear apart the married life of Yance and Josué as their swings move in opposite directions, one rising while the other falls. Raphaël's brutal dominance and eventual sexual initiation of Marie-Christine, on the other hand, sets in motion a complicated series of events that will end in her eventual domination of him, as he is content to follow in the wake of her theatrical success.

In the encounter of the two couples, a line has been crossed, and, in the terms of the text, the children seem condemned to enter a painful adulthood. If childhood is unhappy in Blais's early work, it is nevertheless preferable to the doomed world of adult relationships:

> Marie-Christine croit avoir abandonné toute sa vie dans cette journée limpide. Elle est un cri vivant et sa solitude pèse à son ventre et à ses

seins. Et cette solitude elle-même est inconnue. Yance regarde Josué. Il a
préféré le brouillard à ses paroles. Il a préféré la rivière à son amitié, mais
Yance veut protéger ce garçon. . . . Il y a deux petites filles déçues dans le
soir. Les illusions tombent comme les feuilles mortes. [Marie-Christine
felt that she had yielded up her whole life during that transparent day.
She was a living cry, and her solitude lay now like a weight on her belly
and her breasts. Yet even her solitude was unknown to her. Yance looked
at Joshua. He had preferred the fog to her words. He had preferred the
stream to her friendship, yet Yance felt the need to protect him. . . . Two
little girls stood disappointed, in the dusk. Illusions fall like dead leaves
to the ground.] (18; 14)

Les Voyageurs sacrés

Published in the same year as *Le Jour est noir, Les Voyageurs sacrés* seems
inspired by the same lyrical reflection on the tragedy of human love and
passion. Edmund Wilson compared its "symphonic and unconventional"
form with Alain Resnais's avant-garde film *Last Year at Marienbad,* with
which Blais's novel shares an intensity of focus (Wilson, 152). The short
narrative never departs from its focus on the couple of Miguel and
Montserrat as they struggle to deal with Montserrat's sudden and overwhelming passion for the brilliant young concert pianist, Johann van
Smeeden, who also exercises a strange fascination for Miguel. The calm
love shared by Miguel and Montserrat, dating from their common childhood in Spain, cannot survive the ravages of a newborn passion, and
Miguel throws himself into the Seine as Johann leaves for his home in
Vienna, leaving Montserrat tragically alone.

As *Le Jour est noir* had refused to situate itself in time and space, *Les
Voyageurs sacrés* points to its grounding in the structures of European culture. The earlier text flows freely from one doomed couple to another; in
contrast, the poetic prose of *Les Voyageurs sacrés* is contained within a
form determined by the movements of the Mozart concerto Johann is
playing as the final drama unfolds—*allegro vivace, allegro ma non troppo.*
This pattern is doubled by a series of different moments—*premier instant,
deuxième instant, intermède, dernier instant.* Through a series of flashbacks
that take place during the concert, the events are also structured by the
passing of time, determined by the days of the week that intervene
between the failure of Miguel's play on the first Sunday and Johann's
final concert on the next.

The week is punctuated by the visits of Miguel and Montserrat to the great Gothic cathedrals of Chartres, Bourges, and Reims, before their return to Notre Dame in Paris. While the setting of *Le Jour est noir* had been defined only by its somber atmosphere, the story of *Les Voyageurs sacrés* unfolds against a background saturated with history, art, and religious symbolism. The magnificent constructions of the Middle Ages evoke thoughts of human mortality and even of their own destruction: pointed reference is made to the fires that have ravaged Chartres and the collapse of one of the towers of Bourges. Even the image of the young French king triumphantly crowned in Reims calls forth images of another child wounded by a crown of thorns and finally crucified. Against the background of the cathedrals, the personal tragedy of Miguel and Montserrat takes its place in the universal drama of birth and death that provides a conclusion to their own story, as Miguel's suicide is juxtaposed to the birth of Johann's child.

L'Insoumise

Published in 1966 in the wake of Blais's literary triumph with *Une saison dans la vie d'Emmanuel*, *L'Insoumise (The Fugitive)* found critics expecting a sequel to the chronicle of Jean Le Maigre. But while it shares with Blais's earlier novels a critique of the myth of the ideal family, *L'Insoumise* marks a radical shift in focus and style. In the early novels, Blais's characters had lived out their troubled passions in a dreamlike world in which the physical setting served only to provide a symbolic mirror of their inner state. In contrast, *L'Insoumise* takes as its setting the most mundane of modern daily lives—the reality of the middle-class housewife. This was not the first time this subject matter had appeared in literature, as Gilles Marcotte has observed,[3] although it was new in Blais's work. Blais's hallucinatory vision creeps into this apparently tranquil family through the diary of the oldest son, a student at the local university. As is usual in her work, it is the youthful characters who have the greatest access to ways of thinking that undermine conventional expectations. *L'Insoumise* is thus the first of Blais's novels to integrate her dark, poetic vision of human reality with the realistic world of everyday middle-class life—a project whose possibilities she would develop in works like *Le Sourd dans la ville* and *Visions d'Anna*.

Blais has called *L'Insoumise* a novel about "appearances,"[4] a term that recurs in her work of this period to take its place as the title of the third volume of the autobiographical trilogy she was soon to begin writing.

The "appearances" to which she refers are both the socially created image of the ideal family that the parents seek to project and the knowledge, limited to partial appearances, that one person may have of a loved one. The accidental death of a young man forces the three people who love him—his mother, father, and best friend—to confront the hypocrisy of their own unexamined lives and the impossibility of knowing another human being. Their perspectives are developed in three successive internal monologues that progressively uncover the hidden existence of a young man who nevertheless remains enigmatic at the end of the novel. Except for the event of Paul's death, which occurs rapidly and offstage, the action of the novel is psychological, as each of the other characters moves toward greater self-understanding and a realization of the unknowability of others. In the poetic world of *Le Jour est noir,* unbearable solitude expresses itself in action: parents abandon children, husbands abandon wives or commit suicide as they become aware of their inevitable isolation. In the world of psychological realism and social respectability presented in *L'Insoumise,* emotions remain beneath the surface, perceptible only in the characters' internal conversations with themselves.

The longest and most developed interior monologue is that of the mother, Madeleine, who has epitomized the image of the bourgeois housewife until her discovery of her son's diary brings her face to face with the hidden truth of his life, as well as her own. As she reads his diary, she has the sensation of waking up to a new reality that defamiliarizes the objects of her daily life. Reading her son's intimate thoughts, she becomes aware that the incommunicative young man who had seemed interested only in sports was capable of a passionate relationship with an older woman and had been haunted by the fear of going off to war. The atmosphere of the war in Vietnam, which continued as the novel was being written, penetrates the otherwise timeless world of the characters through Paul's persistent dream of being taken off to be killed in a mysterious and morally troubling conflict. His haunting visions of tearful departures and crowded trains, from which young men are dragged off to be killed, links his anxiety to concentration-camp images of World War II.

Paul is also obsessed by his relationship with the mysterious Anna, a rich older woman whom his mother sees as an impossible and idealized love. Reading Paul's diary, Madeleine is reminded of her own long-concealed infidelity to her husband and finds herself passionately identifying with her son's revolt against the moralizing domination of his father, against whom she has never dared to affirm her own opposition. The realization that she has been living a lie does not lead her to action, but it does enable her to resist the self-image constantly imposed by her husband in order to form impressions of her own.

With the news of Paul's death in a skiing accident, the narrative focus abruptly shifts to the father, Rodolphe, who must confront the fact of his son's ultimate escape from his authority. Rodolphe's interior monologue begins with an assertion of smug insensitivity that at first seems to corroborate his wife's observations. Faced with his son's death, he can feel only resentment at the repeated evidence of Paul's disobedience to his will: he sees Paul's willful departure on the fatal skiing trip, against his father's wishes, as one more sign of his son's refusal to submit to his own plans for his life—definitive proof of his lack of love. As he slowly comes to terms with his son's death, however, this respectable doctor is awakened to a more nuanced perception of reality—a vision of which his wife has long thought him incapable. He even begins to perceive his own limitations, realizing, as she has already observed, that he is capable of seeing only one aspect of things at a time.

Rodolphe's reflection on the overt rebellion of his son forces him to recognize the barely perceptible signs of Madeleine's profound resistance to his authority, revealed in her veiled sympathy for Paul. He, too, realizes the extent to which he has been content with appearances, like his wife, valuing above all the image of the happy, prosperous family:

> Nous étions un couple très uni aux yeux des gens. Et cela comptait pour moi. Les petits étaient beaux et bien vêtus. Nul pli de nos difficultés de vivre n'apparaissait. L'honneur de bien paraître, et de paraître heureux, était intact. [In the eyes of others, we were a truly united couple. And that was important to me. The children were well dressed and carefully washed and brushed. There was not a wrinkle in our appearance to betray our inner troubles. The esteem that a healthy, happy appearance always inspires remained intact.][5]

Through his reading of Paul's diary, Rodolphe discovers, as his wife has already done, that what he has known of his son has only been a misleading appearance. As Madeleine's penetration into the hidden reality of her son had changed the appearance of her world, her husband also begins to see things in a new way, the reassuring surfaces of ordinary household objects suddenly revealing hidden terrors. As he begins to perceive the concealed reality of Madeleine, he resigns himself to the knowledge that he will never really know his wife or any other person:

Je disais "ma vie," "ma femme," mais la menace de la mort, proche ou lointaine, m'inclinait à penser que si Madeleine avait été à moi, cela n'avait duré qu'un instant et qu'elle-même avait repris son don, son amour, et que j'avais repris les miens aussi, d'une manière différente, préférant souvent à elle tout ce qui n'était pas elle, et souvent, aussi, tout ce qui n'était que moi. Je comprends qu'il en était de même pour toute chose en ce monde et j'éprouvais moins de tristesse à penser que je ne possédais rien, sinon de rapides apparences de tout cela que j'avais tant aimé. [I spoke of "my life," "my wife," but the threat of death, whether far or near, inclined me to believe that if Madeleine had once been mine, it had been for no more than a fleeting moment and that she had reclaimed the gift of her love, just as I had reclaimed my own, though in a somewhat different manner, often preferring anything that was not even related to her, or anything that was not related to myself, for that matter. I understood, however, that I was not unique in this respect, and I felt less sorrow at the thought that I possessed nothing but fleeting reflections of all that I had loved so dearly.] (217; 79–80)

But as the story of his wife's secret infidelity begins to unfold before his eyes, Rodolphe is distracted by the discovery of another kind of love, his son's relationship with a male friend. As his wife had been fascinated by Paul's passion for an older woman, perhaps seeing in it an idealized version of her own relationship with her son, her husband becomes obsessed with the friendship Paul had enjoyed with his running companion, Frédérik. Seeking to penetrate the secret of their intimacy, the father has a brief glimpse of the world of homosexual desire when he discovers a note in which Frédérik laments Paul's inability to return his love. Later, looking for Frédérik in the cold streets of the city, he is confronted with the ostracism to which this unconventional desire subjects the young man, who has been symbolically orphaned. When he finds Frédérik lying in the snow after being beaten up by a band of hoodlums, he sees his son's friend, like the young men killed in war, as another victim of the violence of society: "dans ce Frédérik nocturne et désespéré, je voyais le jeune homme fusillé avant l'heure" ["in that desperate nocturnal figure, I caught a glimpse of a young man shot down before his hour"] (215; 78).

In the third interior monologue of the novel another layer of appearance is peeled away, as the narrative briefly enters the reality of Frédérik to explore his hopeless love for another man. Frédérik relives his intimacy with Paul, nourished by books and sports, and interrupted only by the arrival of the beautiful Anna, to whose desire Paul responds as he has been unable to do with Frédérik. Deprived of his love even before Paul's death, Frédérik, through his grief, is able to comprehend the parallel solitude of Paul's parents, and his lonely fate provides a final vision of the inevitability of human isolation. Frédérik's confession, as well as Rodolphe's fascination with him and with the possible homosexual dimension in his son's life, brings to bear on the myth of the traditional family another reality it conspires to hide while, at the same time, introducing the marginalization to which homosexuals are subjected in the inhospitable and hypocritical society Blais portrays.

Although it begins by situating itself in the familiar world of the middle-class family, *L'Insoumise* penetrates this deceptive surface to reveal a nightmarish reality not far removed from that of Blais's early work. The novel uses the events and settings of everyday life as the space for her continuing exploration of the tragic quest for intimacy undertaken by beings condemned to solitude.

Le Loup

After exploring the breakdown of relationship within the traditional family in *L'Insoumise,* Blais focuses in *Le Loup (The Wolf)* on human relationships that fall outside the limits of social convention: homosexual love between men. Although homosexuality had entered her work in the adolescent embraces of Jean Le Maigre and his brothers and, more openly, in the troubled passion of Frédérik in *L'Insoumise,* this is the first of Blais's texts in which love between men becomes a central focus. As it is perceived through the eyes of the young protagonist, Sébastien, homosexual relationships are neither a source of perversion nor an object of erotic titillation but a natural expression of human love. He sets forth his position at the beginning of his first-person narrative:

> Je veux parler dans ce récit de l'amour des garçons pour les hommes, des hommes pour les garçons, pourquoi ne pas dire plus simplement "de l'amour de mon prochain," car le monde des hommes qui aiment les hommes est le seul prochain que j'aie profondément connu ou du moins que j'espère mieux connaître pendant mon existence. C'est le prochain que j'ai choisi. [I want to tell you about the love of boys for men and of men for boys—or, quite simply, about "love for my fellow creature." For the world of men who love other men is the only one that I know intimately, or that I hope to know better during my lifetime. I have chosen my fellow creature.][6]

Victor-Laurent Tremblay has argued convincingly that the structure of *Le Loup* is based on musical forms, specifically the form of the fugue.[7] The "art of the fugue" is associated with the composer Johann Sebastian Bach, whose work is also suggested by the name of Blais's protagonist. A musical structure is appropriate to this story, in which almost all the characters are connected to the world of music: Sébastien is a concert musician; Eric, a composer; Lucien, a music professor; and Georges, a patron of the arts. As a polyphonic composition involving one or more voices, the fugue is particularly appropriate to the structure of the novel, which involves a series of unstable relationships in which the participants repeatedly engage in dialogues with each other. In the fugue, as in Blais's novel, the voices function in counterpoint, rather than coming together in the chords of harmony. By maintaining its different voices in a state of constant dialogue, refusing the resolution of harmony, the fugal form mirrors the reality of the human relationships Blais portrays.

Although only 24, Sébastien presents his monologue as an attempt to understand the meaning of his past, "un lourd passé sensuel dont je voudrais pénétrer davantage le mystère et la complexité" ["a highly sensual past whose mystery and complexity I would like to penetrate more deeply"] (10; 7). For Sébastien, the past is the history of his relationships with others, which become a primary source of his identity: "Je n'avais l'impression d'exister par moi-même que lorsque quelqu'un m'aimait" ["I had the impression that I existed only when someone loved me"] (79; 66). As Tremblay points out, the novel's homosexual perspective provides a standpoint from which conventional familial structures can be critiqued, but it functions most importantly as a means of exploring the possibility of human relationships that move beyond the traditional structures based on heterosexual monogamy. Sébastien and his various lovers are presented as different ways of experiencing the homosexual condition: some are destroyed by their inability to confront the condemnation of society, others find happiness in the joyous promiscuity of gay bars, while still others work at creating enduring personal relationships. But beyond the specificity of their mode of living homosexuality, each of Sébastien's amorous encounters explores a more universal problem of human relationships.

The nature of Blais's analysis is suggested by her title, which evokes the saying, "man is a wolf to man." Sébastien's relationships with his lovers play out in various ways this relationship of predator and prey, each of his partners displaying an aspect of this predatory behavior. As his current lover, Eric, accusingly puts it, it is this profoundly human aspect of his lovers that most attracts Sébastien; Eric tells him,

> Vous m'aimez parce que je suis un loup, comme Bernard, comme Lucien, autrement je ne pourrais pas vous intéresser, vous savez que je suis violent et capable de faire du mal aux autres, voilà pourquoi vous persistez à m'aimer. [You love me because I'm a wolf, like Bernard and Lucien; otherwise I wouldn't interest you. You know that I'm violent and capable of hurting others; that's why you persist in loving me.] (135; 112)

This violence takes different forms in each of Sébastien's relationships but in each case he sees it as a symptom of fear, "the animal fear of death," and this insight constitutes for him one of the fundamental mysteries of human relationships:

> Georges, par peur, Bernard, par agression sauvage, oui, pourquoi, me disais-je, deux êtres mis l'un en face de l'autre, plutôt que de se fondre dans un sensible harmonie, ne songeaient-ils qu'à s'entre-dévorer comme des bêtes rivales? [Georges out of fear, Bernard out of savage aggression, yes, I asked myself, why should two creatures think only of devouring one another like rival animals when they were face to face instead of melting into a sensual harmony?] (117; 96)

In Sébastien's compassionate vision, each wolf contains within himself the vulnerability of the lamb. Sébastien dreams of warming with sensual fire the symbolically frigid bodies he encounters. For him, love is evoked by pity, and each relationship represents "une unique expérience de compassion" ("a unique kind of compassion") (10; 8).[8]

In each of Sébastien's relationships, this balance of predator and victim takes different forms. His school friend Bernard is brutal and demanding, alternately threatening violence and abandoning his lover for other bodies. Yet through Sébastien's compassionate vision, Bernard's rage to destroy is exposed as a response to his own feeling of social marginalization, and his need for his friend is evident in his despair when Sébastien departs for the conservatory. Sébastien's patron, Georges, who finances his music studies, takes out on his protégé his fear of his own pederastic desires. For his professor Lucien as well, Sébastien becomes the embodiment of homosexual desires, hated and feared because of the social ostracism they entail. Even his lover, Eric, finally casts him out in his desire to enjoy the exclusive possession of their mutual companion, Gilles.

In his reflection on his experiences, however, Sébastien comes to see that the relationship of mutual devouring is, at the same time and somewhat paradoxically, one of mutual nourishment. Of his imperfect relationship with Bernard, Sébastien is able to say, "Il m'avait nourri et s'était nourri de moi" ["He had nourished me and had been nourished by me"] (85; 70). This process is represented by the scene in which Bernard, in a symbolic gesture with overt religious overtones, offers his naked body as a site and source of nourishment:

> Tu vois, disait-il, je suis tout à fait nu comme une table, si tu m'aimes, improvise un peu pour m'apporter à boire et à manger. Caresse-moi tout le corps avec des pommes, enveloppe-moi dans des fougères, et si tu as faim et soif à ton tour, viens boire, tous mes membres sont à toi. [I'm completely bare, like a table. If you love me, improvise a little and bring me things to eat and drink. Caress my body with apples, wrap me in ferns and if you are thirsty and hungry too, come and drink. All my limbs are yours.] (64; 52)

The communion in *Le Loup* is physical and sexual, and those characters who refuse the contact of the body, like the ascetic Pierre and the fearful Lucien, are associated with the coldness of stone and the aridity of the desert. Yet repeated references are made to the spiritual blood of the sacrificed lamb, and the suffering Sébastien is likened to the crucified Christ as well as to the martyred and bleeding body of his saintly namesake, generally represented with arrows piercing his flesh. Sébastien perceives that his suffering for others may not only possess the power to save them but may become a source of nourishment for himself, perhaps like the monastery that appears in his dreams, a community of men who live on sacrificial suffering: "Ils ne vivaient plus que du rayonnement de la tendresse qu'ils avaient acquise en souffrant pour d'autres hommes" ["They neither ate nor slept, but lived off the outpouring of tenderness they had acquired by suffering for other men"] (13; 10).

In contrast to the image of predatory human wolves, Sébastien glimpses the possibility of a form of reciprocal love between men, an ideal connected with the symbolic house from which he feels forever banished. The image of a possible human fraternity, of mutual compassion rather than mutual destruction, appears to the narrator in his relationships with his many brothers, a vision that recalls the family of Jean Le Maigre:

Nous avions appris à être les uns pour les autres, dans la vie quotidien-nement, non seulement des fils mais des pères (ce dernier rôle semblait même nous convenir davantage): pour survivre, ne devions-nous pas tous nous aider, oubliant, quand nous étions trop jeunes, un âge humain (l'âge des tout-petits, l'ère de la complaisance) qui entravait nos pas vers une liberté fraternelle plus grande? [We had learned to be not only sons but fathers to one another in our daily life—in fact the role of father even seemed to suit us better. In order to survive we all had to help one anoth-er, forgetting when we were too young, a human age (the age of the very small, the era of complacency) that impeded our steps towards a greater, fraternal liberty.] (18; 14)

In this image of mutual parenting, Blais evokes an ideal of human relationships similar to that proposed by the American feminist Adrienne Rich, which she herself embodies in her later work: "It is a timidity of the imagination which urges that we can be 'daughters'—therefore free spir-its—rather than 'mothers'—defined as eternal givers. . . . To accept and integrate and strengthen both the other and the daughter in ourselves is no easy matter. . . . But any radical vision of sisterhood demands that we reintegrate them."[9]

In attempting to embody this ideal on a larger scale, in order to avoid the stifling limitations of the couple, Sébastien hopes to "enlarge the cir-cle" of human relationships in a ménage à trois. But his idealistic experi-ment, undertaken when he introduces his former lover, Gilles, into his relationship with Eric, founders when Eric himself becomes a wolf, devouring everything in his desire for the exclusive possession of Gilles. In Sébastien's vision, the exclusive relationship of the couple is itself a source of destruction, summed up in Eric's description of his own rela-tionship with Gilles:

Je pourrais élargir le cercle jusqu'à vous, vous laisser vivre de façon support-able entre Gilles et moi, mais je ne peux pas. Quelque chose de déraisonnable me pousse à m'enfermer avec un seul être, à l'écart de tous, et d'extraire de lui, goutte à goutte, tout ce qu'il ne peut pas me donner également! [I could broaden the circle as far as you, let you live in some tol-erable fashion between Gilles and me, but I can't do it. Something unrea-sonable forces me to shut myself up away from everyone with one person, and to extract from him, drop by drop, everything he can give me; and what is more evil, that which he cannot give me as well!] (161–62; 133)

Although all of Sébastien's attempts at relationship have failed in the course of his narrative, he himself seems to have gained the sustenance to pursue his efforts:

Peut-être est-ce la vérité, mais il est possible aussi qu'un amour donné sans mesure, même très mal donné, ne soit pas complètement perdu; si cette goutte de sang avait un jour le pouvoir d'abreuver celui qui m'a lié à lui par sa soif et par sa souffrance, alors, oui, j'aimerais y destiner encore ma vie. [Perhaps that is true, but it is also possible that love given unstintingly, even if it is given very badly, is not completely lost; if one drop of blood has the power to quench the thirst of the one who has joined me to him through his thirst and through his suffering then, yes, I would like to dedicate my life to that once again.] (172; 141–42)

Despite the failure of each of the couples described, Blais's view of human relationship in *Le Loup* is less black than in any of her preceding novels. She has envisioned an ideal of human harmony, and her suffering narrator is committed to pursuing his search for compassion and pity, prefiguring the compassionate vision that would come to dominate her work of the late 1970s and 1980s.

Chapter Six

Dramatic Statements:
L'Exécution, L'Ile, and
Plays for Radio and Television

Although Blais's dramatic texts are not numerous, she has returned to theatrical forms throughout her literary career. Three of her dramatic writings have been performed in Quebec. *L'Exécution* was staged in 1968 at Montreal's Théâtre du Rideau Vert. Several years later she contributed a dramatic monologue, "Marcelle," to the feminist collective production organized by Nicole Brossard and France Théoret, *La Nef des sorcières* (Ship of Witches), staged in 1976 (see Chapter 9). Blais did not have occasion to write again for the stage until 1988, when her play *L'Ile* was produced in Montreal by the Théâtre de l'Eskabel. Throughout the 1970s, however, she published a number of radio plays, as well as one play that was produced for television.

Blais's writing for the stage seems to have been at least in part a response to troubling social issues that were preoccupying her at the time, perhaps inspiring her with a desire to enter into direct communication with an audience. Both *L'Exécution* and *L'Ile* deal with problems that demand a collective response, and they implicate the spectators in the events taking place on stage. Written at a time when Blais's notebooks reveal her to be troubled about the American involvement in Vietnam, *L'Exécution* shows the way in which collective feelings of innocence and guilt can be manipulated and deformed by a ruthless and destructive leader. The play's staging of the indifference of a group of boarding-school students to the death of an innocent young classmate suggests a parallel to public indifference about the deaths in Vietnam. More than two decades later, another scandal of collective indifference calls forth a dramatic response: society's failure to respond to the victims of AIDS. In *L'Ile* Blais turns the spotlight on the "tourists" who look on unfeelingly at dying gay men, seeing in their suffering only a source of contamination. And Blais's contribution to the feminist production of *La Nef des sorcières,* a rare act of participation in a collective text, was a response to the need for women, and particularly lesbians, to make their voices heard in the early years of the Quebec feminist movement.

While Blais's stage plays seem related to a need to speak out, her radio and television dramas of the 1970s grow from her preoccupation with communication—or, rather, lack of communication—between human beings. Her radio dramas give substance to the voices that also express themselves in the interior monologues of her fiction of the same period. As with her novels, her dramas focus on the inner lives of her characters rather than on external events. Their failed dialogues under-line the isolation of human beings, a perennial concern of her work. In some of the radio plays, however, as in her dramatic monologue "Marcelle," Blais stresses instead the growing affirmation of a female voice.

L'Exécution

L'Exécution, Blais's two-act play, continued the preoccupation with adolescent violence evident in her novels of the preceding years. Blais termed the 1968 play "a drama of destruction and violence."[1] The pro-duction won praise from Montreal critics, among whom it enjoyed a cer-tain succès d'estime. Its dark and violent subject, however, had little appeal for the patrons of the Théâtre du Rideau Vert, who demanded more amusing plays for the following season.[2]

The plot of *L'Exécution* had been suggested to Blais by an episode that had occurred a few years earlier in a Quebec boarding school, in which three adolescents had been accused of the apparently senseless murder of the school porter (Leblanc, 330). In Blais's version, three boys engage in a Nietzschean plot to commit the gratuitous murder of a 14-year-old schoolmate. But the play moves beyond the concept of the *acte gratuit* to explore the power exerted over others by a cold and ruthless leader.

Although Blais allows her public to furnish their own contemporary parallels, the text is a palimpsest of literary allusions, each suggesting its own mode of interpretation. Several references are made to medieval tales of knightly virtue: Eric, the young victim, is identified with Prince Eric of the children's tale, and the name of Lancelot is given to the one student who insists on defending the truth. Jennifer Waelti-Walters finds this naming a key to the deeper meaning of Blais's text:

> Eric is our Prince Charming, the beautiful, pure and innocent hero who should reign triumphantly over evil at the end of the story. Yet Eric is the

victim of a senseless and bloody murder, and Lancelot is accused of the crime. If we consider first the names of these two characters we see that through their defeat the whole hero tradition, the chivalrous and godfearing search for the good, the beautiful and the holy is called into question, rejected as a code appealing to children only, and a code of ruthless expediency takes its place as man's mode of successful operation today.[3]

Blais also provides abundant references to Greek tragedy. The ruthless Kent has played the role of Oedipus, the king who has gained his throne by killing his own father. He has also played Creon, the pragmatic successor to Oedipus who becomes the murderer of Antigone. Both these roles suggest Kent's fascination with the manipulation of political power. The boys offer the unsuspecting young Eric tickets to a production of *Phèdre,* evoking thoughts of the immolation of another innocent victim of evil; Martin's sister Hélène is busy reading about Electra, sister of another murderer. And, clearly, Blais's reduction of the mass of students to an anonymous group of silhouettes transforms them into a kind of chorus. These classical references, in the context of the play's austere action, certainly encouraged the director, Yvette Brind'Amour, to stage it as a "modern tragedy."[4]

The drama turns around the relationship between the implacable Louis Kent and his conscience-stricken friend Stéphane Martin, appropriately nicknamed "Luther," who are the only two characters of substance in the play. Kent, like his predecessor, David Sterne, is cold and without emotion, basing his personality on the Nietzschean phrase he is fond of quoting: "Ne plus rien accepter du tout, ne plus rien prendre, ne plus rien absorber, n'avoir plus aucune réaction" ["Accept nothing, assume nothing, take nothing in, give nothing out in return"].[5] Kent is constantly associated, as Laurent Mailhot points out, with images of coldness and winter.[6]

In *David Sterne,* her novelistic treatment of a similar character, Blais had allowed the reader to participate in David's gradual refusal of human emotion. In *L'Exécution* her focus shifts from the exploration of a cruel and contemptuous protagonist to a demonstration of his ability to make others carry out his will. Blais thus suggests a second meaning for the "execution" in her title, which refers not only to the killing of the young Eric but also to the execution of Kent's orders. As he states to his classmates, "J'ai pensé à tout. Je vous donnerai des ordres. Vous les exécuterez" ["I've worked all that out. I give the orders, you follow them"] (17; 15).

Kent is able to exert his influence not only over his friends Stéphane Martin and Christian Ambre, who unthinkingly carried out his wishes, but over the collective body of the other students in the school, whom the stage directions describe as silhouettes or shadows. Kent's power to dominate is evident as he persuades the collectivity to affirm their complicity in the murder and subsequently to inculpate the only two students capable of standing up against this group mentality. In the menacing figure of Kent, who bears ultimate responsibility for the death of an innocent, Blais seems to be pointing to the ability of political leaders to manipulate concepts of guilt and innocence to their own advantage.

Even though the play's boarding-school setting makes no explicit reference to current political events, several of the play's readers saw references to Hitler, and another read it as an indictment of the Catholic Church—a continuation of the polemic Blais had begun in *Une saison dans la vie d'Emmanuel*. Blais's own notebooks of the period of the play's composition suggest a reference to contemporaneous events in the Vietnam war, which preoccupied her thoughts throughout this period. Referring specifically to *L'Exécution*, her notebook for 20 February 1968 sees the play's portrayal of the collectivity as related to the collective indifference to Vietnam that Blais observed around her, and to all such collective indifference to suffering.

L'Ile

The small tropical island that constitutes the world of Blais's *L'Ile* is a microcosm of the disintegrating world threatened with destruction that had formed the background of *Visions d'Anna* and *Pierre*. One new factor has been added: an unnamed epidemic that shows all the symptoms of AIDS. In an interview Blais described the setting of the play as "une île que tous les fleáux modernes attaquent, le racisme, le sida, l'indifférence . . . une société en rétréci [an island attacked by all the modern plagues, racism, AIDS, indifference . . . a society in microcosm]."[7] In *L'Ile* death is not merely envisioned as a result of some distant nuclear holocaust or poisoning of the environment, as it is in the earlier works. Here death is imminent and omnipresent, destroying the joyous world of the young couples of gay men who frequent the island's bar.

As Blais has revealed in her memoirs, *Parcours d'un écrivain,* the atmosphere of the play was inspired by the warmth of the people she frequented at a bar named Square One in Key West. Like the island in the play, Key West is an isolated tropical paradise with a heterogeneous population made up of elderly women, gay men (Key West, like Provincetown, is a well-known center of gay life), artists and dancers, and various types of tourists, young and old, bikers and bourgeois. For Blais, in her memoirs, the bar offers a haven of human warmth from the terrors of racism and disease that form the background of her meditations. As she writes, "Que deviendrais-je sans cet éclairage attrayant et nuancé, cette objective chaleur qu'ils interposent entre le pessimisme ou le simple réalisme de mes pensées quant à l'évolution de l'humanité et leur climat de joie, d'aération estivale et candide? [What would become of me without this attractive and nuanced lighting, this objective warmth that they interpose between the pessimism or the simple realism of my thoughts about the evolution of humanity and their climate of joy, of summery and open lightness?]" (*Parcours*, 95).

The main action of the play takes place on Christmas Eve, beginning with animated preparations for a party and continuing throughout the night, as the island's inhabitants gradually disappear. According to the stage directions, the play opens with a crowd of characters in a lively bar and ends with a deserted stage. The island's bar, like many others, is dominated by a video screen, but this one functions to bring into what should be a site of joyous celebration images of a hospital, in which a dying gay man and his lover watch videos of their formerly beautiful bodies harmonized in dance. The video images repeat the atmosphere of decadence and decay that pervades the play, as, according to the stage directions, erotic images of beautiful bodies are slowly deformed before the spectator's eyes, just as the joyous atmosphere of the bar itself, at first full of patrons preparing to celebrate Christmas Eve, is, in the course of the play's action, transformed into a lonely and desolate place.

The traditional meaning of Christmas morning as a time of joyous rebirth is subverted by the relentless progression of death. The blond baby Jesus of the local Christmas pageant is identified with black ghetto children destined for death. The last scene, showing a young gay dancer holding his dead lover in his arms, is especially significant, as it runs counter to the nativity scenes appropriate to the season. Instead, it suggests a Pietà, the image of Mary holding the crucified Christ.

Although its effects are recognizable and ever-present in the play, AIDS itself is never mentioned as the source of the deaths that are slowly depopulating the island, shutting down its sumptuous resort hotels that have been the symbolic scene of a liberated gay life. After building a house together, Jim and Dave see their lives being slowly eaten away by the discovery of Jim's disease, as their home is being slowly devoured by tropical ants. Unable to respond to the loving gestures of his companion—or to the camaraderie of his friends in the bar—Jim finally sets himself adrift in the ocean on a raft, as he has earlier symbolically isolated himself on a float in the pool. The fate of Jim and Dave is mirrored in the couple of dancers, Denis and Jean, who vainly try to continue their dancing career as Denis becomes progressively weaker. At first he appears walking with a cane, but soon, visible only in video images, he is confined to a hospital bed, unable to move.

Like *L'Exécution, L'Ile* shows the influence of Greek tragedy in its unrelenting focus on the inevitable movement toward a tragic conclusion and also in its brief recourse to the device of a chorus. The unnamed onlookers who form the chorus are explicitly identified as "tourists," visitors from the world outside, and the coldness of their contempt forms a shocking contrast to the human warmth that still provides a temporary refuge from the overwhelming invasion of death. A couple turns back from entering the bar when they recognize the nature of its clientele, and they smugly remark that such people are segregated at home to avoid possible contamination. At the hotel pool, in which Jim floats listlessly, the tourists gather to surround him with their disgust, refusing to enter the water. It is their attitude, as one of the older men comments, that keeps those afflicted with the disease virtual prisoners in their own homes, from which they fear to emerge.

But AIDS is not the only menace to the lives of the marginal beings who inhabit Blais's island. The black male prostitute Jerry drugs himself to calm the rage that still possesses him after his childhood rape by a priest. Like the good-looking young black man who is the protagonist of Blais's short story "L'Exilé," Jerry has been refused a job playing the piano in the resort hotel, being relegated instead to the invisible world of menial work. Jerry is literally and symbolically a source of contagion in the island, as he opens it to the drugs and violence of the black ghetto in which his young cousins have already been killed, falling victim to the same social forces from which he tries to protect the young drug pushers on the island. These adolescents spread their own contagion to a group of young women motorcyclists who congregate in the bar, one of whom overdoses in the bathroom.

Some of the island's inhabitants are simply dying of old age, which the elderly Tony compares with the debilitation of the young AIDS victims. But in Blais's world death can be put off by the human warmth of the group in the bar as it is with Cookie, the old alcoholic abandoned by her son, who is fed and sheltered by her friends. When the son appears to take her off to a nursing home for detoxification, she is transformed from an active if eccentric old woman into an immobile figure sitting stiffly by a barred window, who has lost all desire to eat and drink. Harmless old women like Cookie are as much the outcasts of the "tourist" society as the AIDS victims whose contamination they fear: as the tourists worry about AIDS contamination of their bathing water, the bohemian Cookie is shown being bathed and disinfected before her admission into the nursing home, where the old are kept from contaminating the rest of society.

Luckily, Cookie can be rescued and brought back to the island by Rose, another eccentric old woman who is as close as anyone in this play comes to playing the role of ministering angel, like Judith Lange in *Le Sourd dans la ville.* A doctor who has dedicated her services to the poor black residents of the island, Rose still devotes herself to rescuing the birds whose oil-soaked wings prevent them from flying. These birds become emblems of the human inhabitants of the island, called in the play "an island of diseased birds." Rose is able to do some good, as she brings Cookie back at the end of the play, but the joy of her return is dimmed by the discovery of the young drug victim in the bathroom.

In this play there is no happy ending, nor can there be. The inhabitants of the island can only try to create an atmosphere of human warmth that makes the inevitable confrontation with death somewhat less solitary. If Blais's play has a message, it lies in its condemnation of the moralistic and self-centered attitudes of the "tourists," who have allied themselves with the many forces that are destroying human life on the island of the earth.

Plays for Radio and Television

The period following Blais's great literary success with *Une saison dans la vie d'Emmanuel* in 1965 was one of experimentation with form. In short fictional works like *David Sterne* and *L'Insoumise* and even, to some extent, in the dialogues of *Le Loup,* Blais played with the use of different voices. The plays she produced for radio and television from 1971 to 1977 represent an extension of her work with this dimension of literary form.

Although radio plays had largely been supplanted by television drama in many cultures by the early 1970s, in the wake of Quebec's Quiet

Revolution and its preoccupation with the French language, the production of radio plays was strongly encouraged by the government-sponsored French-speaking Radio Canada. Radio offered writers an opportunity for the diffusion of dramatic works in French to a wide audience without having to contend with the economic exigencies of Montreal theater companies, some of which still preferred the classic French plays over the work of local authors.

In its reduction of dramatic means to the words and intonations of a human voice, the radio play corresponded to Blais's propensity, evident in much of her fiction, to place the emphasis on the spiritual dimensions of her characters rather than on their physical surroundings. In *L'Exécution* Blais had already reduced the mise-en-scène to the bare stage appropriate to classical drama. In shifting from stage to radio drama shortly thereafter, she had only to reduce the participants in the drama to the two or three characters who form the core of her short fictional narratives.

In the radio play[8] Blais encounters a form that lends itself to her continuing exploration of the limitations of the couple, the tensions within the structure of the family, and finally, pointing toward the project she would undertake in *Les Nuits de l'Underground* and later works, the affirmation of the voices of women.

The unnamed stranger who enters and destroys the world of a quiet farm family in "L'Envahisseur" (The Invader) recalls the traditional Quebec oral tales, in which a mysterious and fascinating stranger arrives in a village to corrupt the young men and seduce the maidens, only to reveal himself as the devil in disguise.[9] Although he is as seductive as this legendary devil, the stranger in Blais's play wins his success by playing on the psychological vulnerability of this apparently happy and united family, awakening the oldest son's desire for the independent life of the city and the wife's need for attention and sensual pleasure. The father's naive belief in human goodness and his willingness to share his own few resources with passing strangers leaves him open to exploitation. But it is his unquestioned dominance as head of the household and his unwillingness to heed the voices of others, particularly his wife, that leads him to ruin. While Blais's message, if any, is unclear, the arrival of the stranger brings to the surface tensions already present in the large rural family, which, as *Une Saison dans la vie d'Emmanuel* had made clear, had a particular resonance in the context of Quebec.

In "Deux Destins" the difficulties of joining two destinies in the institution of marriage begin to emerge through the action of a catalyzing visit from the husband's old friend Gilbert. In the eyes of the independent Gilbert, it appears that Christine has entrapped Jacques into a mediocre life of financial success and devotion to family, necessitating his abandonment of a promising writing career. His writing has indeed been reduced to random sentences scribbled in haste on bits of paper, and his artistic expression consists of the Schumann piece he plays on the piano every evening with his young son. As Christine finally begins to speak, however, she replaces Gilbert's vision of her husband with her own— that of a mediocre man who is deaf to the voice of others, especially to Christine's. As the dialogue develops, it is clear that both Christine and Jacques have been imprisoned in their union.

It is again the family that is the center of the drama in "Le Disparu," as a family reacts to the unresolved disappearance of the youngest son, who has either fallen into the sea or gone off to seek his own life. Gérard's overt rebellion against the restrictive values of this affluent bourgeois family forces the others into acknowledging the limitations inherent in the father's doctrine of devotion to family and service to others. Gérard's brother Robert, who has fulfilled his family's expectations by becoming a doctor, realizes the emptiness of this ideal as he confronts his inability to feel compassion for his individual patients in his scramble for money and reputation. Gérard's mother sees the way in which she has refused to recognize the individual needs of her sons by forcing them all into conformity with the father's vision of material success and ruthless competition between brothers.

It is Gérard, with his insistence on the value of the individual and the meaning of personal happiness, who has put the traditional pattern in question. In this he resembles the young people of the late 1960s, in Quebec as well as in France and the United States, who were questioning "the establishment" and the value patterns of their elders: "Gérard n'était que cela, la mauvaise graine de la liberté, une génération désordonnée et troublante parmi nous qui étions parfaitement organisés et sans trouble [Gerard was only that, the bad seed of freedom, a disorganized and troubling generation among us, we who were perfectly organized and untroubled]" (54).

Blais's pessimistic vision is not entirely without hope because she allows Gérard's fate to remain unclear. He is imagined leading a bohemian existence not unlike that of the young women in Blais's 1989 novel, *L'Ange de la solitude,* one of whom is also named Gérard. In an imagined scene of Gérard's return, however, Blais makes it evident that the others have no hope of escape. The father, whose imposition of authority has led his sons to ruin, remains unmoved, while the mother and Robert are paralyzed by their own contradictions. Unable to join Gérard in his new life, Robert leaves for a walk on the same perilous rocks where his brother had presumably met his death.

Four of Blais's radio plays were published, along with a text written for the stage, under the title *Sommeil d'hiver* (Winter Sleep) in 1984. The title play, never produced on stage, is also in some sense a reflection on the relationships of women and men. The Dead Man, the main character, has momentarily come back to life and desperately seeks human companionship. But in the women who come to his side he encounters the failures of his life, his lack of courage, and his inability to respond to the needs of others.

Each of the four radio plays—"L'Exil" (Exile), "Fantôme d'une voix" (Ghost of a Voice), "Fièvre" (Fever), and "Un couple" (A Couple)—consists of a dialogue—perhaps intersecting interior monologues would be a better description—between a man and a woman. Although the situation of each of the couples is different, in each case the woman's voice is struggling to free itself from domination by the man's. This focus is entirely in harmony with the program of the feminist publishing house, Les Editions de la Pleine Lune, which affirmed itself as "an instrument at the service of women's voices."

In "L'Exil" a wife laments her long exile in a cold authoritarian country. Not unlike the former Soviet Union, it is a country where art is censored and writers are shut up in psychiatric hospitals. Although the woman shares her husband's opposition to the regime, her fate seems identified with that of the writer in his underground hiding place and the people heard singing in the church, who will soon be crushed by soldiers.

In "Fantôme d'une voix" the voice of the woman has begun to affirm itself, entering into real dialogue with that of the man. The voice of the title is not only the one in which she (Elle) expresses her newfound sense of self but also the singing voice that had paradoxically first attracted her husband, who had then forced her to abandon singing in order to devote herself entirely to his career as a composer. As an old man he is now capable of listening to the voice she is beginning to rediscover through her own music notebooks.

As she attempts to write music that would capture the unique qualities of a female voice, the woman meditates on the reflections of a male composer, who prefers to write for the simple voices of young boys rather than women, because women's voices are complicated by feeling:

"quand la femme est sensuelle, sa voix trahit cette sensualité, cette richesse intérieure, ou cette volupté de vivre [when the woman is sensual, her voice betrays this sensuality, this interior richness, or this voluptuous pleasure in living]."[10]

In her search to recover her voice from the silence that has obscured it for so long, the woman identifies with the multiple voices of women of the past who have suffered the same fate:

> Une voix, ce n'est peut-être que le fantôme d'une voix aujourd'hui, après tout ce temps à vivre près de lui. Je pense souvent aux femmes du passé, à toutes ces voix qui ont longtemps dormi. Autrefois, cela devait être si dur, on attendait de nous une telle patience, un tel stoïcisme, un tel silence. [A voice is perhaps only the ghost of a voice today, after all this time spent living with him. I often think of the women of the past, of all those voices that have slept for a long time. In the past, it must have been hard, we were expected to have such patience, such stoicism, such silence.] (85)

But she takes heart from the solitary courage of Emily Dickinson and the artistic testimony of the Renaissance painter Fede Galizia, whose voice she seeks to prolong:

> Je pense à ces grands peintres de la Renaissance, des femmes comme moi, elles croyaient ne pas avoir de noms, d'histoire, des voix que l'on croyait mortes, oubliées je les entends, je les vois, rien ne meurt je renais. . . . Fede Galizia dont la voix, sur cette terre, fut si silencieuse, si contenue, un murmure, mais elle vit parmi nous, cette voix, j'imagine son histoire, son combat solitaire, tout ce temps entre elle et moi, et elle vit encore près de moi. [I'm thinking of those great Renaissance painters, women like me, they thought they had no names, no history, voices that were thought dead, forgotten I hear them, I see them, nothing dies I am reborn. . . . Fede Galizia whose voice, on this earth, was so silent, so contained, a murmur, but it still lives among us, this voice, I imagine her story, her solitary struggle, all this time between her and me, and she still lives near me.] (97)

In "Fièvre" another long-married couple, identified only as Man and Woman, experience a rupture in their uneventful relationship while traveling in North Africa. It is through her speaking that, apparently for the first time, the Woman is able to affirm a vision of reality that conflicts with that of the Man. In this strange and exotic country she becomes suddenly aware of another world that threatens their self-enclosed bourgeois existence. The situation is somewhat reminiscent of Albert

Camus's short story "The Adulterous Woman," in which a woman traveling in the desert with her husband is symbolically seduced by the freedom and austerity of the Bedouins. The Woman in Blais's drama encounters a world of suffering and social injustice, evident in the contrast between the vacationing Europeans and the hungry people who surround them, and in the sumptuous gardens from which the poor are excluded. Like the male adolescents of *David Sterne,* the Woman yearns to experience the life of the masses around her, as she says, to experience their suffering to the fullest.

Although the medium is sound, images of vision dominate the text. The Woman realizes that she has seen life only through the eyes of her husband; her image has symbolically been captured in the lens of his camera. To see for herself, she must walk alone. But her efforts to go off on her own are complicated by her fear of unknown paths and her long-established patterns of dependency, as well as by moments of affection for her husband. As the dialogue ends, it is not clear what she will do, but she vows not to lose the insight she has gained: "Mes yeux sont ouverts. Ils ne se refermeront plus [My eyes are open. They will not close again]" (138).

In "L'Océan," a play produced on Radio Canada television on 28 May 1976, the family drama springs from the overpowering presence of a writer-father, completely absorbed in his art and, in his later years, in the sensual experience of living. For him, writing is an effort to master the forces of life, to become the sole creator of his destiny. As Blais indicated in *Parcours d'un écrivain,* his character is based on a man she knew in Cape Cod, who gave up a concert career to compose music he refuses to sell or even to communicate to others, much to the despair of his wife. In Blais's play the composer, in his single-minded preoccupation, not only neglects his devoted wife but destroys his children. His daughter Maria, revolting against her mother's enslavement to love, marries a man to whom she is indifferent, refusing her passion for Nicolas, another rejected son of an artist. The writer's son Simon has taken his revenge on his father by becoming a literary critic, coldly dissecting literary works to reveal their hidden flaws. Another son, François, whose own efforts to write have been mocked by the father, has nevertheless chosen to share his father's alcoholic isolation. As in "Fantôme d'une voix," the figure of the artist as great man is inevitably selfish and destructive to those around him. In his self-absorption, he is not far different from the nonartistic patriarchal figures of "Le Disparu" or *L'Insoumise.*

In "Un couple" and in the later radio play "Murmures," the male-female dialogue is not so much a struggle for dominance as a confrontation of two incompatible attitudes toward life. In "Un couple" the young Françoise fights to preserve the freedom of the bohemian life she has shared with Jean-Pierre even after they become parents. As he encloses her in a small apartment, she accuses him of accepting the life of older generations, betraying their youth with rigid structures. She dreams of carrying their son around on her back, creating a new generation that would share in the freedom of birds. Jean-Pierre, on the other hand, is haunted by apocalyptic visions of the future. He sees their generation represented not in the free flight of birds but in a Dutch painting of a girl with death standing over her shoulder. Where Françoise sees the sensual pleasure of life on the beach, he sees beaches polluted by oil, and he focuses on boys who torture seagulls for their pleasure.

In their opposing visions of life the two characters represent a new generation's polarized responses, which in a different register are repeated by the brother and sister of "Murmures." While Judith is haunted by the transitory nature of life, her brother Luc finds happiness in caring for the suffering of the world, in his work with handicapped children. It is these competing responses to life that are to some extent reconciled in the character of Judith Lange in *Le Sourd dans la ville,* who is able to combine a tragic vision of life with a devotion to suffering humanity. As Paula Gilbert Lewis has pointed out, Judith in the play uses two voices—one that she addresses to Luc and another to express her innermost thoughts to herself[11]—a technique that is also important in Blais's novels, where the characters' unspoken words are often set in counterpoint to their spoken dialogue.

Chapter Seven

Portrait of the Artist as a Young Girl: *Manuscrits de Pauline Archange*

Shortly after publishing her dark parody of a mythical rural Quebec in *Une saison dans la vie d'Emmanuel,* Blais began to work seriously on a long-contemplated project, the story of a young girl living in an urban setting much like the one in which she had spent her own childhood. In the pages of Blais's Notebooks of the late 1960s, it is evident that her original project of writing a sequel to *Une saison dans la vie d'Emmanuel* was being displaced by the intrusion of childhood memories, her own or those of her protagonist, Pauline Archange, and it is her effort to follow this source of inspiration that leads her into the longest sustained project of her writing career, the three-volume series entitled *Manuscrits de Pauline Archange (The Manuscripts of Pauline Archange).* The three novels appeared in rapid succession between 1968 and 1970, the second and third bearing the French titles *Vivre! Vivre!* and *Les Apparences (Dürer's Angel).* Together they tell the story of Pauline Archange as she progresses from early childhood to a precarious adult independence. *Manuscrits de Pauline Archange* is at the center of Blais's attention in the closing years of the 1960s and signals the beginning of a more personal era in her writing, in which her work is grounded in the structures of contemporary reality rather than the mythical and poetic worlds of the early novels.

Although Blais continues to examine the problems she had begun to treat in *Une saison*—the difficulties confronting the young artist and the repressive forces of the surrounding society—here the target of her attack is not the idealized rural Quebec of the *roman de la terre* but the lower-middle-class Quebec City in which she herself had grown up. *Manuscrits de Pauline Archange* is the story not of an imagined *poète maudit* who tragically dies young but of a young girl who is destined to succeed in writing the narrative of her own life, as is suggested in the closing words of the first volume:

> Née dans le récit même que je voulais écrire, j'aspirais seulement à en sortir. Ce qui me désolait le plus, c'était de penser qu'il était si long, si dur

pour moi de vivre, et que dans un livre, cela ne prendrait que quelques
pages, et que sans ces quelques pages, je risquais de n'avoir existé pour
personne. [Born into the very story I wanted to write, I aspired only to
find a way out of it. What made me feel most desolate was the thought
that it was such a long, such a hard business for me to live, and that in a
book it would take only a few pages; yet without those few pages I was in
danger of never having existed for anyone.][1]

The three volumes of *Manuscrits de Pauline Archange* are Blais's portrait of
the artist as a young woman. They are also as close as any of her writing
has come to autobiography.

Although Blais has on occasion disavowed an autobiographical connection, it is hard to deny that Pauline Archange has much in common
with the young Marie-Claire Blais. The eldest of several children, Pauline
Archange lives in an unnamed city that is easily identified with the
Quebec City of Blais's own youth. Forced by financial necessity to cut
short her education at the convent school, she nevertheless persists in her
determination to become a writer, despite her parents' opposition, supporting herself in a series of low-paying jobs. Whether or not certain
characters and episodes of the novel were taken from Blais's own life, in
its essential points the experience of Pauline Archange repeats the trajectory of Marie-Claire Blais. It is as if the process of writing about Quebec
in *Une saison dans la vie d'Emmanuel,* with its distanced, parodic perspective, along with the freedom of living outside of Quebec itself, had given
her the physical and emotional distance necessary to look back at her
own life.

Her direct inspiration for this project was, in fact, the experience of
living in the poor black neighborhoods of Cambridge and Boston in the
early 1960s, where she saw the relationship between the racial oppression apparent in the United States and the class oppression she had experienced in the Quebec of her childhood. As she later described this
period,

Je tente d'écrire bien maladroitement encore, dans un roman sur les dif-
férences sociales, ce que je pourrais avoir vu de comparable à la situation
des Noirs dans la société québécoise, . . . le monde des usines où j'ai vu
tant de jeunes vies s'étioler, s'éteindre pour toujours. [I am trying to
write, very clumsily still, in a novel about social differences, what I might
have seen in Quebec society comparable to the situation of blacks . . . the
world of factories where I have seen so many young lives wither and die.]
(*Parcours,* 32)

It is her heightened consciousness of the nature of this oppression that accounts for the bitterness of tone that pervades the narrative:

> Les mots qui me viennent pour décrire l'abaissement d'une classe sociale par une autre (à la fin des années cinquante, au Québec, où une classe est nettement prédominante sur l'autre, celle des patrons sur les ouvriers que rien ne protège et qu'un despote qui gouverne avilit même davantage) sont ternes, ils ont le ton même de la douleur renfrognée que je ressens. [The words that come to me to describe the debasement of one class by another (at the end of the 1950s in Quebec, where one class is clearly dominant over the other, the bosses above the workers, who have no protection and who are debased even more by a tyrant who governs) are colorless, they have the same tone as the sullen grief I feel.] (*Parcours,* 32)

More diffuse than *Une saison dans la vie d'Emmanuel* and lacking the earlier novel's sharp satirical edge, *Manuscrits de Pauline Archange* was not immediately perceived as a political statement, although certain critics welcomed its attacks on the convent schools, to which almost all Quebec children had been subjected in the era before 1960, when all education was still in the hands of the Church. When *Manuscrits de Pauline Archange* is compared with a highly politicized male autobiography of the same era, the difference becomes clear. Pierre Vallières's *Nègres blancs d'Amérique (White Niggers of America),*[2] published in 1967, is the explicitly autobiographical account of the life of a lower-class boy in the newly developing suburbs of Montreal. As is evident from his pluralized title, Vallières envisions his autobiographical persona as representative of the people of Quebec: his singular experiences are meant to be emblematic of a collective reality. As is also indicated by the title, his perspective on this experience is clear: the people of Quebec, as represented in the young protagonist, share the economic exploitation and ethnic inferiorization also experienced by African Americans.

As we now know, a similar analogy betwen Québécois and black Americans provided the point of departure for Blais's book, but this perception is not made explicit in her novel. Nor, unlike Vallières, does Blais situate her protagonist's life in an explicit political and sociological context (although to Quebec readers who had participated in the contentious political debates of the 1960s, this context might have been evident). Lurking behind the large, often tubercular families who overrun the poor sections of the city, and the unexplained hostility between parents and children, is the harsh reality of the demographic policies advocated by the Quebec Catholic Church and enforced by the government's strict ban on family planning. And this is also the unstated reason that a mother too sick to care for her existing children and a father worn down by long hours of work nevertheless continue to expand their family, even though they can no longer provide for their teenage daughter, who is forced to cut short her education to take a series of humiliating and poorly paid jobs. Although it also goes unstated, the severe repression of sexuality and, indeed, of all bodily functions can be seen as part of a larger policy that submits human sensuality to the society's reproductive concerns.

Poverty is apparent in the life of Pauline Archange, but class differences are not often visible, since she has little opportunity to escape from her own limited milieu. Only as she peddles calendars door to door is she allowed to penetrate into the homes of the rich bourgeois who are usually hidden from her eyes in this hierarchical society. Pauline's friendship with an invalid girl she meets on one of her calendar-selling expeditions becomes a source of humiliation for Pauline's mother, as her own children's poverty becomes exposed, and she points out the inappropriateness of Pauline's friendship with the daughter of the local doctor. Poverty exists in the novel, but the reasons for economic exploitation are unstated. Only when her friend is dismissed from her after-school job in a large department store does Pauline come face to face with economic inequity and injustice. And later she realizes, as her father comes home from work chilled to the bone, that his boss can afford to own three automobiles but is unwilling to spend money heating his factory.

What Pauline does perceive, in the incomprehension of the woman doctor who tries to befriend her as well as in the unreality of the literature produced by an intellectual elite, is that there exists a wall of indifference that effectively renders invisible the lives of the poor. Unlike Vallières, Blais makes no investigation into the larger causes behind such inequities. No hostile Anglophone presence is visible in this uniformly Francophone world of Quebec City, and only rarely does Pauline's vision penetrate to the upper levels of power. Only once, in a ceremony held in the Quebec Coliseum, does she perceive the magnificence of the purple-robed bishops and listens to her affluent friend, Julien Laforêt, proclaim his desire to participate in the power shared by the political and clerical leaders. Blais's critique is grounded in the personal experience of Pauline Archange, a protagonist incapable of gaining a perspective on the society as a whole, and the economic exploitation and political oppression she undergoes is interwoven with the elements of her own individual character, which, however, has been formed by this milieu.

As critics have remarked, women autobiographers are noted for their tendency to focus on events that belong to the private sphere rather than the public. In this sense Blais's work is like other women's autobiographies. It bears a particular resemblance to the explicitly autobiographical work published a few years earlier by the Quebec writer Claire Martin. Martin's two-volume *Dans un gant de fer (In an Iron Glove)* puts evident emphasis on her childhood oppression by an excessively patriarchal father. Although Martin does trace some of the lines that tie her father's apparently aberrant behavior to a larger system of repressive social values, her focus is clearly on the personal and private rather than the public and political.

The autobiographical narratives of both these Quebec women writers of the 1960s share a common structure: their protagonists progressively reject the authoritarian demands of those who dominate their lives and, by the end of the stories, they have achieved a level of personal autonomy.[3] Although their stories are never explicitly related to events in the Quebec political realm, the personal liberation that structures these autobiographical works clearly corresponds with the collective political movement of Quebec in the 1960s, from an initial questioning to a progressive dismantling of outmoded and authoritarian structures of religious, political, educational, and familial institutions.

The way in which this most personal of Blais's literary texts intersects with the political reality of Quebec at this time is enlightening. It perhaps suggests an answer to the question of why women writers like Gabrielle Roy, Anne Hébert, and Blais have achieved positions of such centrality in the Quebec literary canon. The feminist writer and critic Nicole Brossard has articulated this question: "Why were their works able to reach a wide section of the Quebec public? With what collective schizophrenia did their own phantasms connect? On what oppression did they throw light?"[4] It was Blais's participation in the sense of shared oppression that permeated the Quebec consciousness at this time that accounts for the resonance her work had for its Quebec readers.

If the sense of oppression evident in the three volumes of *Manuscrits de Pauline Archange* spoke directly to her readers, other elements of their construction left them open to criticism. Many of those who responded favorably to *La Belle Bête* and *Une saison dans la vie d'Emmanuel* were taken aback by what they perceived to be a certain formlessness in the rambling trilogy. One reviewer warned, "It is futile to seek either logic or chronological order."[5] It is true that, in contrast to Blais's best-known previous work, *Manuscrits de Pauline Archange* places little emphasis on plot. Although the three volumes are generally organized by Pauline's progression from childhood to maturity, Blais's focus is on the episodes of daily life that constitute the texture of Pauline's experience. Unlike *La Belle Bête,* the story of a female childhood constantly invaded by violence and death, the sporadic events of *Manuscrits de Pauline Archange* include the commonplace experiences of moving to a new house, a visit to the country, a firemen's parade. For this reason it is a story difficult to paraphrase, and one reviewer found it to be a novel where "nothing happens,"[6] a perception heightened by the absence of events of political or historical significance.

As her focus on the personal rather than what has traditionally been labeled political places her in the company of other women autobiographers, the same can be said of the perceived formlessness of Blais's novels. Estelle Jelinek has noted that the narratives of women's lives are "often not chronological and progressive but disconnected, fragmentary," and she speculates that such discontinuous forms may tend to mirror the "fragmented, interrupted and formless nature of [women's] lives."[7] Because women's autobiographies often fail to conform to the criteria of "orderliness, wholeness or a harmonious shaping" (Jelinek, 19), Jelinek and others have argued for a broader definition of the autobiographical form—one that might include memoirs as well as diaries and letters, forms long used by women to give words, if not shape, to personal experience. In the terms of new critical explorations of women's autobiography, even a collection of essays like Blais's 1993 *Parcours d'un écrivain* could claim recognition as an autobiography, as indeed it should. And these theories allow the "formlessness" of the Pauline Archange trilogy—which so disconcerted Quebec critics on its appearance—to be placed in some perspective.

In fact, there is a discernible structure in Blais's text, and that structure is the result of the protagonist's interaction with the other people who form her life. Such a focus on relationships with others is, in fact, another feature that has been seen to be common to many autobiographical works by women. Mary G. Mason, among the first to note this trait, observed that "the self-discovery of female identity seems to acknowledge the real presence and recognition of another consciousness, and the disclosure of female self is linked to the identification of some 'other.'"[8] For Domna Stanton, the creation of the subject of women's autobiography is related to the process of female development outlined by feminist thinkers such as Nancy Chodorow and Carol Gilligan: "The female 'I' was thus not simply a texture woven of various selves; its threads, its life-lines, came from and extended to others."[9]

These observations are borne out by such central texts of women's autobiography as Simone de Beauvoir's *Memoires d'une jeune fille rangée,* a text explicitly shaped by the young girl's relationships with her parents, with her friend Zaza, and later with Jean-Paul Sartre. The stress on relationships with others that feminist literary critics have found in women's autobiographies would seem to bear out the findings of much recent work on female development. In particular, Nancy Chodorow's influential *The Reproduction of Mothering* emphasizes that, perhaps because of the intense nature of the mother-daughter relationship, a woman's sense of self is extended to others and that, unlike men, who are taught to value individual autonomy, women experience themselves in relationships.

In Blais's trilogy Pauline Archange's relationships with others are profoundly ambivalent. Her family life inspires her to revolt against her parents' arbitrary authority. At the same time, it awakens her to the mute suffering of those like her mother and her cousin Jacob, whose lives are submerged by the forces of their milieu. Although she instinctively refuses to identify herself with the frail and doomed creatures who surround her, it is their lives she is inevitably compelled to describe in her writing.

In her search for other, more forceful models for her life, Pauline turns toward the older woman Germaine Léonard, who, in an era of limited opportunities for women, has carved a career as a doctor and a life of independence from marriage. Yet even this exemplary female figure is bound by the prejudices of her milieu, which prevent her from finding fulfillment in love or real compassion for those, like the young Pauline Archange herself, whom she seeks to help. Especially in *Les Apparences,* where Germaine Léonard moves to the center of the story, she is placed in contrast with the fascinating and contradictory figure of the priest Benjamin Robert, whose intense compassion is inextricably bound up with his need for sexual contact. Although Germaine Léonard condemns the nonconformist priest for indulging his homosexual desires in his intimate relationships with convicted criminals, Benjamin Robert's ability to enter into the world of his fellow men provides an illuminating contrast to her own limited understanding of human suffering.

As in *Une saison dans la vie d'Emmanuel,* Blais is particularly hard on the institutions of her society—family, school, and church—all dominated by a life-denying religious doctrine that Blais's readers quickly recognized as typical of pre-1960 Quebec, which has often been called the period of the *Grande Noirceur* (Great Darkness). Even in the first volume of the trilogy, where events are seen through the eyes of a five-year-old child, the world of the novel is characteristically dark and, at times, horrifying. Proust's influence is evident, especially in the convoluted sentence that opens the trilogy:

> Comme le choeur de mes lointaines misères, vieilles ironies que le temps a revêtues du sourire de la pitié (une pitié puant légérement la mort), les religieuses qui, autrefois, berçaient ma vie de leur cruelle bonté, m'épient encore au grillage d'un cloître perdu dans la fade campagne, sous un ciel mécontent, au bord de la tempête, mais qui accueille comme un encens maladif la plainte de leurs prières, de leurs cantiques au Saint-Sacrement. [Like the chorus of my distant miseries, ancient ironies clothed by time with a smile of pity (though a pity that faintly stinks of death), the old nuns, who once cradled my life in their cruel kindness, still keep their eyes on me through the shadowy grilles of a cloister buried in the colorless countryside, under a sullen sky, at the fringe of a storm, but perpetually receiving, like a sickly incense, the lamentation of their prayers, of their hymns to the Blessed Sacrament.] (11–12; 3)

But the childhood world of Pauline Archange holds none of the magic experienced by Proust's Marcel, with his sunlit promenades in the countryside punctuated by moments of ecstatic contemplation before a hawthorne hedge. If it is a luminous natural beauty that alerts Proust's protagonist to the synthesizing power of his imagination, the material that offers itself to the young Pauline is far different. In the end, however, she realizes that it is in this world that she will have to seek her salvation, as she says, "descendre dans cette cave de boue et de feuilles séchées, pour regarder une dernière fois ces vivants et ces morts dégénérés d'où il fallait tirer, plus que la naissance, plus que la vie, ma résurrection" ["to go down into that depth of mud and dried leaves to take a last look at all the living and the degenerate dead from whom, more than my birth, more than my life, I had to extract my resurrection"] (184; 93).

No childhood paradise, the world of Pauline Archange is peopled with sadistic nuns who reek of cabbage, poverty, and avarice. Small children wander lost in freezing streets, prey to lascivious men who try to lead them off to dubious adventures. Even their homes fail to offer a safe haven: adults are pictured as insects, endlessly reproducing to their own dismay, or as moles, who emerge timidly from their holes to call in their recalcitrant children. Blais's mothers seem intent on strangling their frail offspring as they knot woolen scarves around their necks.

The systematically degrading vision of the child/narrator approaches the parodic stance of *Une saison dans la vie d'Emmanuel* during Pauline's brief summer vacation with relatives in the country—a sort of return to the Quebec past. A suggestion of the hallucinatory unreality of life in the country à la Blais appears in the name of the rural town Saint-Onge-du-Délire (formed on the model of real Quebec place names), which even its own residents have trouble finding in the labyrinth of indistinguishable dirt roads. Pauline's country relatives consist primarily of children crippled in body or mind, and, like her rebellious cousin Jacob, these unfortunate beings are crushed into nonexistence by the brutality and incomprehension of their environment. Jacob stands up to the constant whippings of his father only to lose the force of his revolt in the mental institution to which his family consigns him. Pauline, too, risks losing the force that will permit her own survival—her ability to see beneath appearances—as she is temporarily blinded by Uncle Victor's whipping.

The random whippings and beatings so much a part of life in the country are rationalized and systematized in the civilized world of the city: Pauline's world is dominated by a sense of judgment and punishment. The severe pronouncements of the "eye of God" described to her by the nuns are echoed in those of her "inquisitor" parents. Her world is burdened with judgments that suppress the struggle for independence in those who, like Pauline, are determined to survive. This is evident from the first words of the text, the meandering and often humorous portrayals of the nuns who preside over Pauline's religious education:

> La joue jaunie par les veilles, leurs petits yeux courant comme des billes dans la lune contemplative de leur visage, leur front trahissant (frivolité secrète) une noire mèche de cheveux drus qui tremble fièrement au seuil de la coiffe, elles suspendent au carreaux de leur couvent . . . cette expression de mépris que connaissent bien les mauvais élèves dont je fus: "Pauline Archange a désobéi, nous la priverons des restes de notre pain d'hostie." [Cheeks sallow from nightly vigils, their little eyes wandering like marbles across the meditative moons of their faces, each forehead betraying like some secret frivolity its dark lock of thick hair, quivering proudly beneath the edge of the coif, they display at their convent's mysterious windowpanes . . . that expression of contempt so familiar to the bad pupils among whom I was numbered: "Pauline Archange has been disobedient, she must be deprived of the leftovers from our altar bread."]
> (11–12; 3)

In the eyes of this religious teaching, the body is perceived as a source of sin and an occasion for punishment: schoolchildren are refused permission to use the bathroom, as an exercise in mortification. Especially condemned are the signs of female sexuality: adolescent breasts are suppressed, and menstrual blood is labeled by the nuns as a punishment from God.[10] Pauline observes, "Il devait être bien terrible d'aimer puisque mes parents en avaient si honte! Mère Sainte-Gabrielle d'Egypte elle-même parlait en frémissant de dégoût" ["It must be terrible indeed to love people, since my parents were so ashamed of it! Mother Sainte-Gabrielle d'Egypte herself would quiver with disgust as she spoke"] (182; 92).

The world perceived by the child is systematically degraded by Blais's sharp prose, in a procedure that often comes perilously close to caricature. When one of the nuns sees in each of the falling snowflakes a soul in the hands of God, the child/narrator goes on to envision the frozen washing hanging from the clotheslines as "âmes raides, encore vêtues de leur chemise de nuit" ["stiff souls still wearing their nightdresses"] (107; 54). As Pauline Archange's piercing vision works to undermine the pious teachings that constitute the major part of her education, at home and in the convent school, her friend Louisette Denis condemns the Catholic doctrine on which they are based as a pack of lies. The failure of an idealizing religion to make contact with reality is constantly underlined by a process of ironic juxtaposition. As the school principal announces an epidemic of infantile paralysis that threatens their very lives, the children mindlessly repeat their catechism lesson about the infinite goodness of God. Particularly chilling is the mental institution in which Pauline's troubled cousin Jacob is confined and finally driven to madness: the nuns go off to torture themselves with prayer and self-flagellation, leaving the patients they are supposed to care for to cry out from hunger and cold.

Even as she undermines the Catholic doctrines of her own Quebec childhood, Blais also reappropriates some of this religious semiology for her own purposes. This is most evidently suggested by the name of her protagonist, Pauline Archange, which she has chosen to emphasize in the title that encompasses all three volumes of the trilogy. The archangel Pauline is the first of Blais's explicitly angelic figures, to be continued in the figure of Judith Lange of *Le Sourd dans la ville* and the enigmatic figure of "the angel of solitude," the title of a later text. Pauline's little friend Séraphine is, of course, also an angel, her name recalling the biblical seraphim, who are traditionally represented as having the face of a child surrounded by three pairs of angelic wings. As the seraphim are identified in the Christian tradition with the fervor of love and associated with the passionate color red, it is with Séraphine that Pauline Archange first experiences passion, which reddens their pale cheeks as the two children roll in the snow. Séraphine is described as a martyr whose soul is so pure that, in the words of one of the nuns, even before dying she falls into the arms of the angels.

Ironically, however, the angel into whose embrace Séraphine falls is "L'Archange Pauline." It is through Séraphine that Pauline Archange first learns she is a fallen angel, an aspect of her character implied by her first name, which suggests the sinfulness constantly evoked by the Pauline vision in the New Testament. While her teachers have condemned her proud disobedience, her family—particularly her suffering mother—has leveled a much more serious judgment: she has no heart. It is through Séraphine that Pauline first hears a demand for eternal love:

> Séraphine . . . s'arrêtait à chaque pas pour être embrassée, demandant qu'on l'aime toujours, plus que le ciel, plus que la terre, éternellement en ce monde et au paradis où nous serions côte à côte si nous avions la chance de mourir le même jour. [Séraphine laughing as she stopped at every step to be kissed, to insist on being loved forever, more than the sky, more than the earth, eternally, in this world and then in heaven, where we would always be side by side if we were lucky enough to die on the same day.] (22; 9)

But, lured away from her frail and pathetic friend by the robust Mireillettes (a form of Girl Scouts), Pauline is forced to recognize the inconstancy of her own love, as well as her self-protective indifference to the suffering of others. When Séraphine, abandoned by her friend, is crushed under the wheels of a bus, Pauline realizes the full extent of her betrayal, as well as the inadequacy of human love in this fallen world.

Pauline's relationship with Séraphine repeats, in another register, her feelings for her mother, debilitated by an unnamed illness. Racked by vomiting, her mother barely has the strength to look after her small children. While the frailty of her mother awakens her compassion, as has Séraphine's lice-ridden head, it also prevents her from identifying herself completely with this relationship:

> J'éprouvais alors une pitié rebelle pour cette femme jeune, déjà atteinte dans sa santé, brisée par le travail, dispersant vite mes pensées toutefois dans une rêverie glacée où elle n'aurait aucune part, craignant de me

laisser émouvoir par ce front pâle penché sur ma page éclaboussée
d'encre, craignant, plus que tout, de rompre notre fragile lien de pudeur
et de silence, par ce geste de consolation qu'elle attendait de moi, lui con-
firmant ainsi que nous n'appartenions pas à la même race meurtrie. [At
such moments I felt a rebellious pity for this young woman, already failing in health and worn out by work, and was forced to drive away such
thoughts with some cold and invulnerable daydream in which she could
play no part, for I was afraid to let myself be moved by that pale brow
bent over my ink-splotched page, afraid, above all, of snapping our fragile bond of reticence and silence by making the consolatory gesture that
she was expecting of me, and thus proving that we did not belong to the
same martyred tribe.] (36; 16)

But if Pauline Archange must deny compassion for others in her daily
life, it will provide inspiration for her writing. Like Blais's earlier writer-
protagonist Jean Le Maigre, Pauline has to struggle against a hostile
environment, but like Blais herself she seems destined to survive, to
assert a precarious independence and take up her career as a writer. The
trilogy has the making of a writer as its structuring principle. Even in
the first volume, which recounts her early years, the little Pauline
Archange has begun to use her imagination as a way of resolving the
conflicting forces of egoism and compassion for others:

> Et dans cette réclusion de chaque soir, je rassemblais peu à peu les frag-
> ments de ma vie, mon imagination écrivait de fougueux récits pendant
> que mon corps feignait de dormir. [And little by little, each evening in
> my solitary confinement, I gathered together the fragments of my life;
> my imagination wrote wild and passionate stories while my body feigned
> sleep.] (154; 78).

As yet unable to manipulate words, the child can create only in the
visual medium of dream, but already her dreams are peopled by the
helpless figures of her mother and her cousin Jacob, who call out to her
creative powers:

> Jacob revivait, minuscule image d'une misère que je n'aimais pas revoir.
> Et ma mère qui avait toujours eu si peu d'existence pour elle-même, ne
> vivant toujours que pour les autres, sortait de l'ombre comme un portrait
> inachevé et l'absence de ses traits effrayés semblait me dire: "Achève cette
> brève image de moi." [Jacob came back to life, the minuscule image of a
> wretchedness I had no wish to see again. And my mother, who had
> always had so little existence in her own eyes, never having lived except

for others, my mother emerged from the shadows like an unfinished portrait, and the void where her frightened features should have been seemed to be saying: "Finish this brief sketch of me."] (154; 78)

The opening scene of *Vivre! Vivre!* stages the ambivalent nature of Pauline's response to the suffering of others through the juxtaposed perspectives of protagonist and retrospective narrator. As her moving van passes the house where the dying Julia Poire smiles at her from behind the bars of her windows, the young Pauline pretends to ignore her while her eye records every detail of the scene. The older narrator is aware of the deeper ambiguity of her position: even as the writer has become deeply involved in the suffering of others, at the same time, she feeds off their suffering by appropriating it as material for her own imagination:

> Les yeux, les paupières, les mains de ces êtres que mon regard avait touchés tant de fois, fondant en eux pour saisir leurs pensées intimes, comment pouvais-je m'en séparer maintenant qu'ils devenaient pour moi les yeux, les mains de créatures volées en secret pour mieux vivre d'elles? [How could I part from the eyes, the eyelids, the hands of these beings my gaze had rested on so many times, melting into them in order to seize their secret thoughts, how could I separate myself from them now that they were becoming for me the eyes, the hands of beings I had secretly stolen in order to nourish my own life?"] (13; 110)

And, in fact, the funeral homes where she has taken refuge with the martyred Séraphine provide the subject matter of her first poems, just as her own suffering and the suffering of those around her will surely provide the matter for the autobiographical project she proudly announces to Germaine Léonard.

It is the child's early attempts to transform her inner world into writing that constitute the central subject of the second volume, *Vivre! Vivre!* Her father's stories about the snowstorm that preceded her own birth inspires her to attempt to possess it:

> Avec la même ardeur, j'écoutais les récits de mon père, croyant posséder un jour, à travers mon langage propre, cette immense tempête que soulevaient les paroles de mon père lorsqu'il me racontait pour la centième fois, avec les mêmes mots simples "la féroce tempête du jour de Noël au temps où t'étais encore dans le sein de ta mère," récit qui semblait refléter dans un passé lointain, un peu de la fureur désolée que j'éprouvais dans le présent. [It was with the same ardor that I listened to my father's stories, thinking that I myself, once I could transmute it into my own language,

would one day inherit that vast tempest blowing through his words as he told me for the hundredth time, in the same simple words, about "the terrible blizzard on Christmas Day when you were still a baby in your mother's womb," a story that seemed to reflect, in a distant past, something of the desolate fury I was feeling in the present.][11]

In her own rewriting of the story Pauline is freed from the restricted space of the familial womb and goes off, alone and fearless, into the night. Yet, in this act of taking possession of her father's story and her own life, she is haunted by a feeling of betrayal.

For Pauline Archange, to live is to write, and her struggle to find time alone with her notebook is an essential part of her effort to preserve her existence. She quickly learns that the price of her writing is an egoism condemned by her family and that even she begins to perceive as a denial of the existence of others. Wholly caught up in her reading as she is supposed to be watching her young brother and sister in the park, Pauline is struck by the extent of her self-absorption: "à l'ivresse de lire en plein air, loin de tous, s'ajoutait soudain un inexplicable enivrement de soi, . . . si moi j'existais davantage, mon frère et ma soeur, eux, n'existaient plus" ["for over and above the intoxication of reading in the open air, away from everyone, I was also feeling a sudden and inexplicable intoxication with my own being, with self; . . . when I myself existed more than ever before, my brother and sister on the other hand no longer existed at all"] (65; 138). But she knows that without this she cannot survive, and she continues to brush off her sick mother's pleas for help with the words, "J'ai pas l'temps. J'écris" ["I haven't the time. I'm writing"] (86; 150).

While Pauline can harden her heart to her mother's need for help and understanding, her father's demands present a more serious obstacle to her efforts. In a symbolic episode, he flies into a rage when she borrows items from the household to use as props in a dramatic production for the neighborhood; he wreaks havoc on her stage sets in order to reclaim his prized beaver hat. Later he condemns her for using up expensive notebooks too quickly as she struggles to put her inner life into words. She is able to recognize these attacks as a consequence of her father's poverty-filled life: "il exprimait ainsi, peut-être, la crainte de l'imagination que je lui inspirais, impatient de détruire en moi ce qui le menaçait en lui-même" ["thus expressing, perhaps, the fear of imagination that I inspired in him, an angry urge to destroy in me what was threatening him, too, inwardly"] (130; 173). Yet she can only strengthen her resolve to avoid being forced into the same situation: "On va pas me manger la laine sur le dos" ["No one is ever going to work the clothes off my back"] (23; 116).

Pauline Archange finds few models for her own work in the literature valued by her society, particularly as embodied in the aptly named poet Romaine Petit-Page. Distanced from the poverty, sickness, and violence of the young Pauline's daily life, Romaine Petit-Page creates a childhood world of lace and golden curls. The disparity between Pauline's vision of the world and that of this poet and her followers is apparent in their response to the falling snow: while the others quote the words of the Quebec poet Emile Nelligan about "la belle neige qui neigeait" ("the lovely snow it's snowing now"), the narrator notes their romanticized perceptions of Quebec reality: "Il neigeait déjà depuis trois jours et de chaque côté des trottoirs s'élevaient des montagnes d'une blancheur suspecte, mais eux ne paraissaient pas s'en apercevoir" ["It had been snowing for three days, and the sidewalks were lined on either side by mountain ranges of less than pristine whiteness, but they did not seem to notice that"] (44; 128). It does not take the young Pauline long to realize that the poet is engaged in creating an artificial kingdom, but she yearns to share in the resources of Romaine's upper-class milieu.

The stories once told around the fire by Pauline's paternal grandmother might provide a better model for her own literary project, but Pauline is revolted by the humiliation of her grandmother's illiteracy: "En tout cas, moi j'serai pas une cruche comme grandmaman qui savait même pas lire et qui signait son nom avec une croix, c'est de la vraie honte à soixante dix ans!" ["Well anyway, I'm not going to be a dumbbell like Grandma who couldn't even read and signed her name with a cross"] (134; 175). In the cultured milieu of Romaine Petit-Page and her followers, the young Pauline is made aware of her ignorance of music and poetry, and she is constantly embarrassed by her inadvertent grammatical errors. Germaine Léonard is also alert to this problem, and as she gives Pauline money to buy notebooks, she instructs her young friend to buy herself a good French grammar. Humiliated by her lack of culture and regarded as inferior even by those who try to help her, the adolescent sees her ignorance as an essential feature of her society, not only preventing her from writing but preventing those around her from putting an end to the social system that condemns a segment of society to disease and hopeless poverty while others are free to participate in the beauty of life. For the narrator, language is inextricably linked to the world of suffering and poverty in which she lives, and she dimly perceives that access to writing offers liberation for her and for her entire world.

As is so often the case in Blais's work, the situation of the writer in this world is summed up visually in a work of art. In the reproduction of Dürer's *Melancolia* hung on the walls of her classroom, Pauline Archange recognizes a representation of a kindred soul, a muscular angel rendered momentarily powerless by his melancholic contemplation of the world before him:

> L'évocation de cet ange vigoureux mais affligé par une lucide impuissance (peut-être parce qu'il voyait au loin ce que moi je ressentais dans ma misère, la cupidité, l'aveuglement des hommes, un horizon voilé de sang— un avenir dont la honte habitait toutes ses pensées, oui, n'était-ce donc que pour ce monde obscur, assassin de la beauté et saccageur de l'innocence, qu'il allait bientôt se mettre à l'oeuvre, lui qui ne désirait que le bonheur des hommes et leur contemplation sans haine?), cette évocation si profonde souffletait pourtant mon courage, enflammait ma foi en une vie supérieure qui fût complètement la mienne sous la forme d'un aveu ou d'un livre, mais contrairement à cet ange prodigieux, si j'avais beaucoup d'énergie pour écrire, je ne possédais pas le don d'exprimer ce que j'éprouvais. [The evocation of this powerful angel, who was at once the symbol of strength and impotence (perhaps because he saw in the distance those very things which I myself so deplored in my misery: cupidity, the blindness of men, a horizon veiled in blood—a future in which shame inhabited all his thoughts, yes, was it not the dark side of the world toward which his gaze was turned as he sat there, the destruction of beauty and dissolution of innocence which he would soon depict in his work, though in his innermost heart he desired nothing but the happiness of men and the ability to contemplate them without hatred?)—this profound evocation attacked my courage, while inflaming my faith in the guise of a confession or a book. But, unlike this prodigious angel, if I possessed the will and the energy to create, I lacked the gifts to express all that I felt.][12]

Dürer's angel is a visual representation of a creative genius, much like Pauline, who is nevertheless linked to the earth and the humble realities of human labor and suffering—a visionary capable of feeling and of transforming her empathy with human reality into a work of art.

Chapter Eight

The Satiric Voice: *Un Joualonais sa Joualonie* and *Une liaison parisienne*

In the mid-1970s, after a long series of introspective and often somber novels, Blais turned a satiric gaze on the world immediately around her: the literary circles of France and Quebec in which she had been enmeshed since the phenomenal success of her first novel. Publishing her book on Quebec, *Un Joualonais sa Joualonie* (*St. Lawrence Blues*), while still living in France, Blais mingled amused caricature with a biting critique of the contemporary literary-political establishment. After returning to live in Quebec, however, she painted an even less sympathetic portrait of Parisian literary circles in *Une liaison parisienne* (*A Literary Affair*).

Un Joualonais sa Joualonie

The protagonist of *Un Joualonais sa Joualonie* is known as Ti-Pit ("Little Nothing"). In her introduction to the English translation, Margaret Atwood describes him as a "Quebecois Everyman,"[1] but he seems even worse off than many of the lower-class heroes abundant in the Quebec novel of this time, having spent his childhood in an orphanage and his adult years working in a series of low-paying jobs. The rooming house where he lives is populated by an assortment of marginal figures—prostitutes, alcoholics, and transvestites—and, if this is not sufficient, his mentor, Vincent, a sort of worker-priest who takes in the dregs of society, provides him even greater access to the suffering multitudes of Montreal. Through a chance meeting in a tavern, Ti-Pit is also admitted into a world of bourgeois intellectuals who range from the nationalist poet Eloi Papillon and his feminist wife to the Marxist militant Papineau to the Quebec City lawyer who makes a fortune writing pornography. The novel follows Ti-Pit as he makes his way through this diverse cast of characters, to produce a series of satiric observations on life in Montreal in the heyday of the Quebec independence movement.

As befits his economic status, Ti-Pit, in his long interior monologue, expresses himself in colloquial Quebec French. As suggested by her title,

Blais seemed to be jumping on the bandwagon of *joual,* a Montreal lower-class dialect that had only recently made its way into serious literature. The term had come into popular use when it appeared in a ringing denunciation of the inferior state of the Quebec educational system under the title of *Les Insolences du Frère Untel* (Frère Untel, Brother So-and-so, was a pseudonym for Jean-Paul Desbiens). In his attack on the lamentable state of the French language in Quebec, Frère Untel defined *joual* as a lazy mispronunciation of the French word for horse, *cheval,* and saw the language he so characterized as proof of the sorry linguistic state of Quebec's children.[2]

Many Quebec intellectuals agreed that the "international French" required in literary expression was not the native language of most French Canadians. The dialect known as *joual,* however, was colloquial *québécois* in its most debased form. As spoken by the working class in the East End of bilingual Montreal, the language known as *joual* was liberally dosed with English, with Anglophone terms for common items pushing out their French equivalents. With bad pronunciation, vowels and consonants often dropped out of words or changed their nature, making even lexically correct French unrecognizable to the uninitiated. In a common transposition, for example, the French word *merde* became *marde* in *joual.* The concept of *joual* also included widely used Quebec expressions, as well as the famous Quebec *sacres,* profanities based on the sacred objects of Quebec Catholicism. For Québécois submitted since childhood to the domination of the Church, the use in profane contexts of words like "chalice" (transposed as *câlisse)* and "tabernacle" (often written as *tabarnak)* held the force of blasphemy.

Responding to the charge made by Frère Untel, the young independentist intellectuals grouped around the journal *Parti pris* were quick to agree on the degraded state of the language spoken by most people in Quebec. But they saw it as a symptom of Quebec's economic domination, its "colonization" by the surrounding Anglophones, English Canadians and Americans. Rather than immediately eradicating the linguistic blight, they advocated the conscious use of the degraded language in literary works as a means of exposing the true situation of the Quebec people. Such a literature, in the poetry of Gérald Godin and the novels of Jacques Renaud, became not only a means of denouncing oppression but also a way to create a bond between writers, traditionally members of a wealthy intellectual elite, and the working masses, the Quebec "common man."

While it was used as a political weapon with some effectiveness by the group clustered around *Parti pris,* young playwrights like Michel Tremblay, who had himself grown up in the East End of Montreal, found it a powerful means of personal expression. Putting on stage people like those among whom he had spent his childhood, Tremblay found it natural to have them speak their own language. The 1968 performance of Tremblay's first play, *Les Belles-Soeurs,* did for *joual* what Lorraine Hansberry's *A Raisin in the Sun* had done a decade earlier for black English in the United States. Embarrassed and sometimes outraged, Montreal theatergoers nevertheless came under the spell of Tremblay's lyrical transformation of the debased language, as he turned *joual* and those who spoke it into the stuff of Greek tragedy. While the use of the language specifically labeled as *joual* was eventually abandoned by those who had adopted it as a political ploy, the controversy it initiated spearheaded a larger invasion of the literary idiom by what has become known as *québécois,* a colloquial language commonly used in Quebec that is related to Parisian French as American is to British English. Particularly in the cinema and on the stage, the use of various local idioms and accents has become an accepted practice.

Still, the ideological debate over *joual* raged for years and continues to flare up sporadically. As works written in *joual* were largely incomprehensible to those outside Quebec, the debate was confined to literary circles in Montreal, and it is these discussions, rather than the creative use of the idiom by writers like Michel Tremblay, that are the object of Blais's satire. The use of *joual* was hardly shocking by the time Blais published *Un Joualonais sa Joualonie* in 1973. Although her own background certainly qualified her to use the language of the "people," her previous novels had made no concessions to colloquial language. Even Jean Le Maigre and his brothers were careful to use a grammatically correct French of a lexical quality comprehensible to a Parisian. If her intention had been to reproduce the speech of the working class of Montreal, she would certainly have been poorly equipped to realize it, having lived only a short time in Montreal and having spent the previous decade in the United States and France. Thus, when she published her first book written in *joual,* her critics, seemingly unaware of any satirical intention, accused her of belatedly responding to a fad. Even worse, they accused her of not writing good *joual,* saying that she put in the mouth of her central character a language actually spoken by no one. They pointed out the infiltration of Parisian terms and the too frequent use of certain endings in -*aille* and -*otte* as a device for transforming standard French into slang.[3]

Somewhat ironically, these critics were accusing Blais of inventing rather than merely transcribing the lively language of her protagonist, and the seriousness with which this charge was made is a testimony to the centrality of the language issue in the political climate of the time. Authors are more often charged with lack of inventiveness than the opposite, and only the concern for authenticity could explain the widespread failure to appreciate Blais's literary game.

But a game it certainly seems to be, and a self-conscious one at that. Blais, indeed, is perfectly aware of the accepted markers of contemporary literary *joual*. Her protagonist has the "typically Québécois" nickname Ti-Pit ("Ti" being a shortened form of "petit"), and he is surrounded by characters named Ti-Guy, Ti-Paul, Ti-Foin, and Ti-Cul—an exaggerated use of nicknames, even for a work written in *joual*. And from time to time Blais indulges in a sentence literally exploding with the borrowings from English so characteristic of literary *joual*: "pendant l'*lunchtime* y lisait des *comics*, t'avais pas avalé ton *cheeseburger* que la cloche nous râlait de partir ailleurs."[4] Or later, "mon *char* . . . il a le *starteur* qui gazouille et le *brighteur* qui s'éteint, quant aux *brakeurs* ils refusent de *stopper!*" (202; my italics).[5] On the other hand, she also makes fun of the militant insistence on replacing all English terms with French: Papillon protests when a waitress offers him "des toasts bacon and eggs" (277) but is then unable to think of the (nonexistent) Quebec French equivalent of "bacon."

Blais's characters even indulge in a limited amount of "typically Québécois" cursing—the famous *sacres,* which draw on the rich vocabulary of a traditional Catholic culture. Thus she reveals herself quite aware of another standard element of literary *joual*. When her unemployed proletarian protagonist meets the poet Papillon, who hangs out in taverns hoping to acquire the local idiom, the first thing that strikes him as odd is the superabundance of *sacres* that color Papillon's speech as he attempts to blend in with the "people": "les Tabernacles, les Ciboires, les Câlices, lui coulaient des lèvres comme des dizaines de rosaires et moé j'pensais: 'Sacrament, y sacre trop, ce gars-là'" ["Hell, this guy curses too much!"] (11; 2). Ti-Pit reacts with sarcasm to this effort to mimic the worst examples of popular speech, and he himself tries to avoid cursing to honor a promise made to Vincent, the worker-priest who had rescued him from the gutter. In this novel only the bourgeois intellectuals use strings of curse words. When Vincent utters a "Jésus Christ" at Ti-Guy's deathbed, the rarity of the expression in his mouth seems to underline the seriousness of the situation.

The frequent literary conversations between Papillon and his editor, Corneille, reveal the extent to which writing in *joual* has become a trend manipulated by a literary establishment at least in part located in Paris. Commenting on the success of the young writer Jojo Cafard, they diagnose it as an ability to produce the right kind of *joual* (*joualon* in Blais's text):

> Il fait du "joual pur" disent les critiques là-bas, et sais-tu pourquoi il est si fort dans son joualon cet adolescent de basse-cour? C'est parce que plutôt que de dire Merde comme on dit à Paris, il dit "Maudite Marde" qui résonne plus largement, selon les joualogues exilés à Paris et ceux qui se prétendent joualogues et qui sont parisiens eux-mêmes. [As the critics over there say, he writes "pure Joual." And do you know what makes that barnyard adolescent's Joual so pure? It's because instead of saying *"merde"* as they do in Paris, he says *"marde,"* which, according to the Joualologists exiled in Paris and the Parisians who set themselves up as Joualologists, has a deeper resonance.] (100; 65)

Papillon admits he himself has been criticized for not writing authentic *joual*—perhaps Blais is wryly predicting the critical reaction to her own novel—but his editor counsels him to be "more Joualonese than the Joualonese" (139), advice Papillon seems determined to follow.

This narrative is clearly conscious of its own relationship to reigning literary fashions, which are constantly the objects of parody and pastiche. The central character, immediately identifiable as picaresque,[6] must also be placed in a more recent tradition of Quebec novels about down-and-out "average Joes"—like Jacques Renaud's *Le Cassé*—or, in a more humorous mode, Jacques Godbout's *Salut Galarneau!* Ti-Pit's transvestite neighbor Mimi and his whole milieu of gay clubs seem to echo the world created by Michel Tremblay in plays like *La Duchesse de Langeais*. Like Ti-Pit, Mimi and his friends are finely drawn, sympathetic characters, and the pastiche is not a hostile one. In fact, although many of the other minor characters remain two-dimensional, it is only the group of bourgeois intellectuals that are satirized with a certain venom.

Un Joualonais has elements of a roman à clef. Many references in the text are thinly veiled allusions to actual phenomena of the time: the Chat Dansant, the tavern where Blais's literati meet the Joualonese, suggests the well-known intellectual rendez-vous, the Lapin Agile; the Parti Rhinocéros, founded by Jacques Ferron, becomes, in Blais's novel, the

Parti de la Girafe. Many of these literary references and in-jokes are lost
on a readership not intimately familiar with the events of the time, but
even where the referent has faded from view, they function as signifers of
the chaotic absurdity of the era.

The nationalist poet Papillon is satirized not only by his name—
French for "butterfly," suggesting the way he flutters around the latest
fads—but also by the contradictions evident in all his magisterial pronouncements. Claiming to be a man of the people, he constantly betrays
the distance that separates him from the life in which Ti-Pit is
immersed. Most of all, he and his editor, Corneille, reveal a calculating
venality in their promotion of the Quebec nationalist cause. Papillon is
deeply offended when his friend, a Quebec City lawyer who has gotten
rich from parking cases, steals his idea for a typically Québécois porno-
graphic novel, in which a young girl is seduced by a priest (the review of
this novel that appears in the text parodies critics who find deep literary
meaning in the most mindless trash). More than the independence of
Quebec, which he so loudly proclaims at every opportunity, Papillon
yearns for a new Cadillac.

Even more viciously satirized than the naive Papillon is his brilliant
former classmate, Papineau. Papineau embodies an entire Quebec radical
tradition, his name recalling the famous nineteenth-century parliamen-
tary leader, while his sons Karl (Marx) and (Jacques) Maritain evoke two
of the major imported currents of the twentieth century, international
Marxist theory and French Catholic existentialism. Like the literati, the
political militant Papineau is undermined by his internal contradictions.
Although he claims to be an advocate of social justice, he is happy to wolf
down huge quantities of Papillon's food, all the while calling him "petit
bourgeois" and "dirty capitalist." And even as he denounces exploitation,
he himself exploits his wife and children in the name of his rigid Marxist
principles, forcing them to spend the harsh Quebec winter in an unheat-
ed tent while he himself carries on an affair with a rich woman. But the
chief failing of Papineau, in Blais's eyes, is his total disdain for human
suffering, which he pompously articulates while his wife is giving birth to
their baby: "La souffrance d'une femme ou celle d'un homme, mais ce
n'est qu'une poussière sur le marbre de nos fronts éternels" ["A woman's
suffering—or a man's for that matter—is mere dust on the marble of our
eternal foreheads"] (108; 71).

Like the thought of Papineau, the political unity of Quebec itself is
portrayed as a mass of conflicts and contradictions. The various groups
who participate in a massive Christmas Eve demonstration of the

oppressed call themselves "les trous-de-cul" or "assholes." But they spend most of their time bickering among themselves until they are finally beaten into an enforced solidarity by the police. The League of Wives and Mothers clashes with the militant feminists led by Papillon's wife, but they disdain Madame Papineau as she struggles with her three small children. Even the nuns fight among themselves, the Sisters of the Modern Rule disputing with the ultra-traditionalists. Longtime Québécois turn against immigrant delegations, especially the "League of Unloved and Disenchanted Frenchmen." The most pathetic case is that of the transvestite Mimi, who, with his blond curls and loud clothing, is systematically rejected by the gay and lesbian groups, moving from the "Common Front of Homos" and "Liberated Sex" to "Power to Sappho" and "Sisters of Bilitis" before he is finally taken in by the "Prostitutes of Québec." The prostitutes' group emerges as the only one unencumbered by some set of exclusive principles. Although they are attacked by the "Bourgeois Wives," they offer food and warmth to the marchers and, as the demonstration draws to a bloody close, they are shown helping out the traditionalist nuns, who mistakenly see them as a kindred group of lay sisters.

Class conflicts, however, are the most pervasive. Workers' groups manifest overt hostility to the students and intellectuals, and Ti-Foin (Little Hayseed), marching with the "Last Farmers of Quebec," tells of the discrimination he suffers even in the radical nationalist groups because of his inability to manipulate language. Papillon makes constant attempts to unify the factionalized crowd with his cry of, "Nous sommes tous des Joualonais unis pour repousser le même agresseur" ["Aren't we all Joualonese, united to repulse the same aggressor?"] (255; 173). But his claims are contested on all sides, and he is finally forced down from the speakers' platform. Blais's portrayal of this march of national unity exposes the emptiness of any claim to an unproblematic Quebec identity, although the bloodied victims of police brutality do establish a form of solidarity in the end. As Atwood comments, "For Blais, ideology separates, suffering unites" (xii).

The element of Blais's book that most undercuts the meaningless nationalist rhetoric proffered by Papillon and Papineau is her portrayal of the underclass of Montreal, among whom Ti-Pit leads his daily life. He quits his factory job at "la Rubber Company" in disgust when his aged co-worker Baptiste is fired without a pension when he develops signs of tuberculosis. But Ti-Pit does not hesitate to condemn Baptiste and his wife for abandoning their son, Ti-Guy, when he turns to drugs as an alternative to being exploited by "la Rubber." The transvestite Mimi is cruelly rejected by his family as he tries to pursue happiness in the clubs of Montreal, and two teenage girls, Josée and Monique, turn to prostitution as the only escape from their overcrowded homes. And, in an act of revenge for childhood oppression, Ti-Pit's orphanage companion, Ti-Cul, returns to murder the farm family who had brutalized them both as foster children.

If Ti-Cul and Ti-Guy represent the destruction and self-destruction resulting from human insensitivity and brutality, the figures of Laurence, Vincent, and Ti-Pit himself offer a more positive response to human suffering. Laurence, a character who seems to be an early sketch of Gloria in *Le Sourd dans la ville,* had distributed love and sex at the orphanage where she worked as a laundress, and later becomes a nonconformist single mother. Vincent, another in the series of Blais's socially conscious priests, has none of the dark underside of Benjamin Robert of *Manuscrits de Pauline Archange.* He combats both his superiors and the irredeemable young dropouts he takes in. Rejecting much of Catholic practice, he cannot bring himself to utter words of religious consolation at Ti-Guy's deathbed. To Ti-Pit's request for the traditional message of Christian hope, he replies bitterly, "Des mots, mais tu te moques de moi! des mots à cet enfant" ["Words . . . such words would be a mockery! words to this child"] (285; 192). In the face of a religion of acceptance he continues a Camusian fight against the injustice of human suffering. As one of his fellow priests sadly comments, "Vous n'aimez pas Dieu au point d'accepter d'être plus ou moins vaincu par la vie, non . . . toujours la lutte sauvage" ["You don't love God enough to accept being more or less defeated by life. . . . With you it's always this wild struggle"] (176; 119).

Vincent's intolerance of insensitivity and hypocrisy and his compassion for suffering are central elements in Ti-Pit's (and Blais's) narrative stance, which alternates between satire and pity. Although Ti-Pit does not claim to be a writer, he does admit to spinning out words inside his head: "J'me fais des fois une jasette pas mal savante mais ça c'est mon secret à moé" ["I have these highfalutin confabs with myself, that's my secret"] (9; 1). The reflection that takes place in his long interior monologue seems responsible for the evolution in his self-image from beginning to end of the narrative. In his opening statement he identifies himself with the name given him by indifferent and contemptuous others: "On m'appelait Ti-Pit, rien que ça" ["They called me Ti-Pit (that's all)"] (9; 1). At the end of the novel, in a dream of a possible future, he insists that Papillon use his real name: "Ti-Pit, connais pas . . . t'as tort,

Papillon, mon nom c'est Abraham, Abraham Lemieux" [Ti-Pit, never heard of him . . . you've got it wrong Papillon, my name is Abraham, Abraham Lemieux"] (301; 203). In the self-affirmation of Lemieux ("the best") and the dignity of the patriarchal Abraham (mixed perhaps with the reminiscence of the Plaines d'Abraham, where the Québécois underwent their first defeat), there is a pride lacking in the self-denigrating "Ti-Pit."

Blais is quick to condemn those for whom the discourse of oppression is merely a literary or political trend, but she is equally concerned with focusing literary attention on the real human suffering of the poor of Montreal, whose problems seem less specifically Québécois than those of *Une saison dans la vie d'Emmanuel* and more related to those common to contemporary Western society. In *Un Joualonais* Blais indulges a talent for amused observation and a need to experiment, however briefly, with colloquial language. More important for her future work, she explores various facets of life in Montreal and begins to develop a narrative consciousness capable of moving around the city and penetrating its various social facades.

Une liaison parisienne

After taking on the Quebec establishment in *Un Joualonais sa Joualonie,* Blais moves on in *Une liaison parisienne* to tackle the literary world of Paris, about which she had learned much during her years of residence in France. Rather than creating a panorama of the entire literary-political scene as she had in *Un Joualonais,* Blais focuses on one particular figure who seems to sum up Parisian values. And for Blais the qualities embodied in the formidable Yvonne d'Argenti are representative of a certain Parisian milieu rather than generically French. As if to make it clear she is not condemning the French people as a whole, Blais shifts her focus completely in the brief last section of the novel to introduce the sympathetic "little people" of France, the human warmth of out-of-the-way Paris bars and the humble integrity of large Breton families, among whom Blais herself had chosen to make her home.

To the young Quebec writer Mathieu Lelièvre, whose name suggests harelike characteristics of wildness and timidity, Yvonne d'Argenti appears to embody all the magical qualities he has so long associated with Parisian life. An established writer, she has access to Parisian literary gatherings, although not of the most enlightening sort. Her best friend, the inappropriately named Mme Colombe (Dove), has made her

money writing pornography, and the attraction she exerts on her followers seems based on her fortune rather than her ideas. The conversation of
these supposed intellectuals is of the utmost banality, and they are clearly moved by material rather than spiritual concerns: at one literary cock-
tail party the intellectuals stalk around the buffet like "fauves d'un
carnage" ["wild beasts around a scene of slaughter"].[7]

Blais's portrait of Madame d'Argenti at the family château demurely
murmuring the platitudes of social respectability and motherly devotion
underlines the hypocrisy of French "traditional values." Behind the social
facade of the typical French family with three lovely children lives another reality: Yvonne and her multiple lovers, the homosexual husband,
Antoine, with his ever-renewed supply of boys, and the neglected children who survive as they can. As Mathieu Lelièvre realizes with respect
to Antoine, the truth of their lives can never penetrate the sophisticated
veneer of their speech: "Non, cela, même annoncé avec élégance, il ne
pourrait jamais le faire, pensait-il, dans une ville, où pourtant sans être
dit, tout se fait" ["No, even if he were to announce it elegantly, he could
never do it, he thought, in a city where, without being talked about,
nonetheless everything was done"] (102; 95).

The hypocrisy that is a hallmark of Yvonne d'Argenti serves to mask
her fundamental materialism, as money (l'argent) is masked by her aristocratic name. Although she speaks of spiritual values and claims to
hunger for the simple country pleasures of Ireland, she pursues a single-
minded quest for the expensive accessories of Parisian life, from designer
handbags to priceless antiques—a quest in which she unhesitatingly
enlists the aid of her various lovers.

Yvonne d'Argenti is portrayed as being such a rapacious, vulgar, and
insensitive person that Mathieu Lelièvre's continued fascination with her
can only be explained by his overwhelming naïveté, itself a consequence
of his uncritical admiration for all that is French. Blais situates her protagonist in a long line of naive observers of decadent French mores: the
critics who review his book immediately label him a "Candide québécois." By means of her protagonist's initial gullibility, Blais creates a double vision for the reader, who cannot help but question the young
Québécois's absurd judgments. His veneration for French culture is such
that when he first meets Madame d'Argenti he interprets her most contemptuous actions, her most vulgar habits, as priceless examples of
French culture. If her furniture is impregnated with cat odors, he can
only see this as proof of an aristocratic disdain for trivial realities: "C'était
cela, pensait-il 'la vraie royauté des aristocrates de l'esprit,' ils ne sen-

taient plus rien" [That, he thought, was 'the true royalty of the aristo-crats of the spirit,' they no longer smelled anything at all"] (26; 26). If he is put to work in the kitchen opening oysters like a servant, he is flat-tered to be admitted to the intimacy of family life. He even comes to see Yvonne's family's lamentable lack of personal hygiene, which shocks even the Portuguese maid, as a mark of their aristocratic attachment to tradition: "Ils étaient au-dessus de tout parfum puis qu'ils conservait l'odeur du passé" ["They were above any perfume because they still pos-sessed the odour of the past"] (30; 30).

In the uncritical veneration of the young Québécois as well as in the condescending and ultimately exploitive attitude of the older Frenchwoman, Blais has produced, as one reviewer suggested, an allego-ry of the literary relations between France and Quebec.[8] In such a read-ing Yvonne d'Argenti, the mother who rejects her children, would be analogous to France, the mother-country that had callously abandoned its Canadian colonies to English domination. Blais had also satirized the exaggerated respect of some Québécois for French culture in *Un Joualonais,* where a particularly obtuse student reveals his standards of literary judgment: "Comme Saint Thomas nous aimons toucher Paris pour aimer l'écrivain de chez nous, autrement nous le méprisons" ["Like St. Thomas we insist on touching Paris before loving one of our writers; if Paris says no, we despise him"] (158; 106).

The Parisians of *Une liaison* do seem to value Mathieu Lelièvre as an exotic phenomenon, but their real lack of interest in Quebec soon becomes apparent. Imagining it as no larger than Brittany, Yvonne d'Argenti pictures Quebec as a country of lakes and prairies where peo-ple have no concept of modern urban life. Even more insulting, she dis-misses Mathieu Lelièvre's interest in the France of his ancestors by saying curtly, "It is not your history." Her real interest in the young writer seems to lie in his money and the presents he can bestow. As a Québécois, Mathieu Lelièvre eventually comes to see himself as one of those excluded from the magic circle of the French elite, identifying more readily with the Breton peasants and even with Antoine's Arab protégé than with the aristocratic d'Argentis.

As the novel proceeds, the young Québécois begins to lose his naïveté, and the humorous double perspective collapses into bitter com-mentary. Thus Blais's novel transforms itself from a Voltairean tale into a nineteenth-century novel of education, in which a young man from the provinces comes to penetrate the mysteries of Parisian life. In an early scene the young writer has just begun to enjoy his oysters while luxuriating in the elegance of Yvonne's apartment, when his impatient mistress brusquely reminds him of the urgency of satisfying her physical desires before her appointment with the hairdresser, thus illustrating her perpetual insistence that "a Paris, on est toujours pressé" ["in Paris one is always in a hurry"] (26; 27). As Yvonne runs off to her next appointment, the young man notices that she has also managed to devour enormous quantities of oysters, wine, and cheese. An initial admiration of this enormous "appetite for life" soon turns into a disabused awareness of her ability to consume everything around her.

The differences in their approach to life become apparent in their writing. Mathieu Lelièvre characteristically displays great sensitivity to his surroundings—his critics call him a "Proustian soul"—but Yvonne closes herself off to anything that falls outside the tightly drawn circle of her own interests. For her, the conversations on which he loves to eavesdrop are only irritating noise. Mathieu Lelièvre notes with surprise that even travel with his mistress is devoid of new sensations because, moving from one French luxury hotel to another, she admits no variation in her habits. For the young Québécois, Yvonne's every gesture seems the culmination of centuries of French tradition, but she is incapable of sharing his passion for the monuments of French history. If she is willing to visit Versailles, it is only because she considers it a fitting background to her elegance: the Hall of Mirrors serves to reflect back her own impeccably groomed image.

The Frenchwoman's single-minded pursuit of her own material desires is not long in revealing its monstrous side. Loudly proclaiming her abhorrence for maternity, Yvonne has rejected each of her three children, forcing her daughter to take refuge in a British boarding school and reducing her hapless son to the status of scullery maid. Her horror of her own children pales in comparison to her contempt for those outside her social circle. A whole history of French racism is suggested in her treatment of the Arab boys who awaken the pity (as well as the sensuality) of her pederast husband, who, as somewhat of a latter-day André Gide, gains favor in Mathieu Lelièvre's eyes as his own limitations are balanced by his compassion for children, including his own, and his persistent tolerance of his difficult and demanding wife. At first impressed by her impetuous wish to go off to help the poor of India, Mathieu Lelièvre is later shocked to hear her saying that an atomic bomb would provide the ideal solution to the problems of Indian overpopulation. Later she dismisses wartime anti-Semitism with the words, "Est-ce qu'on n'a pas le droit de haïr qui l'on veut?" ["Don't we have the right to hate whom we please?"] (137; 126). In her untroubled egoism Madame d'Argenti becomes a repository of all the racial and class conflicts that have divided modern France.

Yvonne d'Argenti functions so effectively to sum up all the criticisms commonly made of the French that it is surprising to learn from Mary Meigs's autobiographical account in *The Medusa Head*[9] that a real person possessed almost all the seemingly exaggerated traits attributed to Blais's character: her domineering nature, her acquisitiveness, her denial of her children, and her pederast husband—right down to the sinister cat who shares her bedroom. The unnamed woman described in Meigs's autobiography had burst into the quiet, artistic lives Blais and Meigs were leading in Wellfleet and had seduced them into moving to France. According to Meigs's account, Mathieu Lelièvre's experiences are in large part those of Blais herself, for whom the writing of this novel served as a form of exorcism. Although Blais has not discussed it elsewhere, her relationship with the real-life Yvonne d'Argenti, as well as the sojourn in France it occasioned, seems to have produced a definitive change in her life and literary production. This change is most visible in her notebooks, in which she had kept an ordered record of her literary and artistic apprenticeship during the Wellfleet years. After the move to France, they suddenly become a disordered jumble of hastily scribbled notes. The writing Blais did during her years in France is characterized by literary experimentation—the search for new subjects and new forms. It was only after she had settled herself back in Quebec in 1975 that she seemed to find a more enduring literary voice.

Chapter Nine

Communities of Women:
Les Nuits de l'Underground
and *L'Ange de la solitude*

The anguish of human solitude that dominated Blais's earlier novels was in her later writings met by a countervailing force—a movement toward the creation of community. These novels may still end with the death of a character and in them the possibility of community can never fully overcome the Pascalian solitude of the individual, but they are also strongly marked by the presence of a network of caring capable of countering the forces of death and destruction. Such a network of mutually supportive relationships, evident in *Le Sourd dans la ville* and *Visions d'Anna,* first makes its appearance in Blais's work in *Les Nuits de l'Underground (Nights in the Underground).* Her 1978 novel, written at the end of a long period of personal turmoil and literary searching, thus inaugurates what I have come to term Blais's mature vision.

Les Nuits de l'Underground is also the first of Blais's novels to be set explicitly in a lesbian context. For Blais, to speak of women loving women immediately implies a movement beyond the individual couple to an entire community of women involved in relationships of mutual caring. While networks of human relationship also constitute the structure of *Le Sourd dans la ville* and *Visions d'Anna,* it is in her two novels focused on lesbian life—*Les Nuits de l'Underground* and *L'Ange de la solitude* (The Angel of Solitude)—that communities composed uniquely of women constitute a collective protagonist.

Les Nuits de l'Underground

Les Nuits de l'Underground begins with a quotation from Vita Sackville-West: "I believe that then the psychology of people like myself will be a matter of interest, and I believe it will be recognized that many more people of my type do exist than under the present-day system of hypocrisy is commonly admitted." With this epigraph Blais places her

text within a tradition of lesbian writing, as she also signals her awareness of its potentially controversial subject matter. Blais's sensitivity to
the transgressive nature of her topic must certainly have been shaped by
her experience in the sexually repressive Quebec culture of her childhood. Only after the Quiet Revolution of the l960s do lesbian relationships find sympathetic portrayal in Quebec literature, in the pioneering
novels of Louise Maheux-Forcier and a few other writers. But it was only
in the course of the 1970s, with the emergence of an assertive feminist
movement, that lesbian writing emerged from the literary margins.

By the time *Les Nuits de l'Underground* was published in 1978, however, the way had already been opened by a number of Quebec women
writers and particularly by the well-known feminist theorist Nicole
Brossard, who had been writing about her own lesbian identity since
1974. Brossard had been a leader of the poets grouped around the journal *La Barre du Jour,* who shared a belief in the need for a revolution in
language that took precedence over revolution in the political sphere. As
Quebec's nascent feminist movement gathered strength in the 1970s,
however, Brossard began to realize the centrality of gender to her work
and to write openly and forcefully about her lesbian identity. Lesbian
writing was not uncommon in Quebec in the mid-1970s, and thus, by
1978, although some Quebec reviewers found Blais's novel polemical, it
seemed neither to shock nor evoke the hostility of the Quebec critical
establishment.

After the publication of *Les Nuits de l'Underground* Blais herself linked
its appearance to the women's movement: "Je suis mon évolution personnelle qui correspond sans doute à un moment important dans l'histoire des femmes [I have followed my own personal evolution, which
probably corresponds to an important moment in the history of
women]."[1] In fact, Blais's first published text focusing on a lesbian was
written as part of a collective feminist enterprise, the landmark dramatic production *La Nef des sorcières* (Ship of Witches) in 1976. This collective creation brought together six short texts written by some of
Quebec's major women writers, including Nicole Brossard and the novelist and poet France Théoret, both of whom also wrote the preface to
the published edition. Such participation in a group project was in itself
unusual for Blais, who had long maintained a fiercely independent
stance. It clearly signaled her willingness to identify herself as a lesbian
and to affirm her participation in the feminist cause.

Marcelle, the lesbian character Blais creates for *La Nef des Sorcières,* is
alone on the stage, as are the five women who appear in the other scenes

(the actress, the menopausal woman, the worker, the prostitute, and the writer). This mise-en-scène is in keeping with the conception of the overall project, which is designed to show the way in which women are isolated from each other. As Brossard and Théoret explain in their introduction,

> Le drame se joue entre la salle et six femmes. Chacune isolée dans son monologue, comme elle l'est dans sa maison, dans son couple, incapable de communiquer du projet à d'autres femmes, inapte encore à tisser les liens d'une solidarité qui rendrait crédible et évidente l'oppression qu'elles subissent et qui les fissure sur toute la surface de leur corps. [The drama is played out between the audience and six women. Each one isolated in her monologue, as she is in her house, in her couple, incapable of communicating with other women, still unable to forge the links of a solidarity that would render believable and evident the oppression they endure, which cracks open the surface of their body.][2]

At the beginning of Blais's monologue, Marcelle hopelessly awaits the arrival of her lover, Lise. Fearing that Lise may have left her, Marcelle laments her incapacity to overcome the fundamental solitude of the individual, to become part of a couple. This is a theme basic to Blais's work from her earliest novels. *La Belle Bête, Le Jour est noir,* and *L'Insoumise* emphasize the isolation of individuals within the couple and within the nuclear family. But in *La Nef des sorcières* Marcelle's solitude leads her to reach out toward other women. Proud of her own self-sufficiency, Marcelle nevertheless admits her need for others: "Même indépendante, forte capable de se nourrir par instants de sa propre expérience, de sa propre vérité, on a malgré tout besoin des autres, pour vous apporter ce qui est différent de vous-même [Even independent, capable of nourishing yourself at times on your own experience, your own truth, nevertheless you need other people, to bring you something different from yourself]" (60–61). Here she is speaking not only of her need for Lise but of her relationships with all her women friends, her lovers as well as those, like Anne, with whom she has no sexual tie (Marcelle's protective relationship with Anne, whom she calls her "brother," is taken up in the characters of Lali and René in *Les Nuits de l'Underground*).

Very much in tune with lesbian feminist texts of the 1970s, "Marcelle" creates a lesbian community of the present and is further linked with a historical community of women loving women, preserved in its own literary tradition: "De tout temps des femmes ont aimé des femmes. Elles étaient comme toi et moi; leurs chants leurs paroles leurs poèmes on les entend encore parfois [Throughout history women have loved women. They were like you and me; their songs their words their poems you can still hear them sometimes]" (61). Recognizing the importance of lesbian writing in providing historical continuity, Marcelle insists on the necessity of speaking about her own reality in order to claim the right to such elementary human gestures as holding hands on the street. As her monologue draws to a close, Marcelle has made the connection between her love for one other woman and her necessary involvement in a network of women who have discovered a form of caring: "Lise sais-tu que tu n'est plus seule sais-tu que d'autres femmes s'aiment quand nous nous aimons [Lise, do you know you are no longer alone, that other women love each other when we love each other]" (63).

The eight-page monologue of Marcelle sets forth the understanding of lesbian community Blais goes on to develop in *Les Nuits de l'Underground*. The novel is structured on a similar movement from solitude to solidarity, a dynamic echoed in the related thematic progressions from darkness to light, from night to day, from winter to spring, from the underground to the open air, from exile to a return to the native land. By its almost-allegorical structure of liberation, the book seems to proclaim its participation in the gay and lesbian liberation movement of the era in which it was written and perhaps also reflects Blais's own sense of personal freedom, combined with her homecoming, a resolution of past conflicts with an oppressive childhood in Quebec.

Although the overall design of the novel tends toward greater openness and freedom, it does not therefore resolve the conflict between isolation and relationship, nor does it erase the difficulties inherent in the couple. Couples are constantly formed and reformed throughout the novel, and, as in her earlier work, Blais continues to portray the relationship within the couple as complex and unstable. Returning to Montreal, Geneviève falls in love with the beautiful but distant Lali, because she resembles a work of art. When Lali moves on to another in her series of intense but ephemeral relationships, Geneviève learns to transform her emotion into sculpture, thus completing the interchange between life and art. She subsequently develops a new relationship with Françoise, an older woman who conceals her sexual identity. Lali's "brother" René (although she is a woman, René prefers to drop the feminine "e") endangers her relationship with the young and devoted Louise by her insistence on pursuing the life of a Don Juan. The generous, outgoing Marielle dedicates herself to the well-being of the group as she recovers from an ill-fated affair. On the other end of the spectrum, the artists

Clara and Ruth, a monogamous couple of an older generation, are separated only by death.

Each of Blais's couples experiences relationship in different ways, but all are involved in a process of mutual caring that also involves the other women in the group, as the group in turn offers its support for the individual couple. The community of women plays an essential role in providing a support network that cushions the failure of relationships between its individual members. As Geneviève has been welcomed into the group when she arrives alone from Paris, her friends support her through the pain of her abandonment by Lali, just as they also support René and Marielle. The importance of this community of women becomes evident when their collective life in Montreal is contrasted with the solitude endured by Françoise as a closeted lesbian in Paris.

The movement from solitude toward solidarity, which dominates the entire novel, is highlighted in the opening scene, where Geneviève is shown sitting alone in the Underground, a lesbian bar in Montreal. She clings to her solitude, but she realizes that, in her newly realized lesbian identity, she has a special need of others: "Une femme pouvait-elle toujours vivre seule, lors que tout, en elle, l'isolait des lois sociales" ["But could a woman live by herself for long when everything inside her made her a social outcast?"].[3] Geneviève yearns to join in the animated conversation of the young women around her but at first finds it difficult to understand their fast-paced colloquial Quebec French after 10 years of living in Paris. Marielle, the first to approach her, also notices the linguistic difference caused by Geneviève's long absence, asking incredulously, "T'es sûre que t'es canadienne-française?" ["You're sure you're French Canadian?"] (3–4).

Like Blais herself, Geneviève had lived far from her native land, and her discovery of solidarity with this group of women is related to her own reintegration into the world of Quebec, a world portrayed as vibrant and relatively free from repression. In contrast, Françoise, a French Canadian who has spent her life in France, has lived in solitude and repression. As Françoise recovers her health and rediscovers her sexuality, it is implied that she will come to Quebec, where Geneviève has decided to make her life. Somewhat ironically, the society Blais once castigated in *Une saison dans la vie d'Emmanuel* for its repression of sexuality becomes in *Les Nuits de l'Underground* the site of potential, if not fully realized, lesbian liberation.

Although Blais had ostentatiously attempted to create a Quebec setting in *Un Joualonais sa Joualonie*, *Les Nuits de l'Underground* is much more convincing in its grounding in the reality of contemporary Montreal. The conversation in the Underground sparkles with colloquial expressions, which seem neither forced nor exoticized, and the women's *québécois* exuberance provides a marked contrast with the Parisian reserve that imprisons Françoise. As Quebec reviewers remarked approvingly, *Les Nuits de l'Underground* is also attentive to its natural setting, evident in the long rides on icy and deserted winter roads, the cold wind that blows the women into the Underground bar. Even the novel's dominant structural pattern—its movement from winter to spring—echoes a long tradition of Quebec fiction, including Blais's *Une saison dans la vie d'Emmanuel.*

Blais clearly identifies the winter landscape with less tangible forces that keep human beings isolated from each other. It is no accident that Lali, who is incapable of commitment in relationship, has chosen to live in an isolated house far from the city, surrounded by miles of snow-covered fields. In Geneviève's vision Lali inhabits a spiritual "polar world" in which "la neige par sa permanence, figeait le sang de la vie sous l'écorce des arbres" ["the endless snow congealed life's blood under the bark of trees"] (237; 176).

During Geneviève's winter in Montreal she observes the way in which her lesbian companions seek warmth in the creation of a world of their own, sheltered from the elements as well as from a hostile society. Blais's novel creates a symbolic "underground" lesbian culture, which, in its separation from the rest of society, allows latent hostility and protest to act themselves out in dramatic episodes. The women gather most frequently in the Underground bar, whose trendy British name signals its below-street-level location. Their other favorite haunt, Moon's Face, is also identified with obscurity and night. Its entry carefully guarded by the muscular Simonet, Moon's Face represents a region of transgression, a "forbidden domain." The women go there when bourgeois families have turned off their lights and gone to sleep; only in a hidden nocturnal existence can their true identities be revealed.

But even these hiding places cannot guarantee protection: the scene of the police invasion of Moon's Face provides an image of the contrast between two worlds, the warmth and solidarity of the women pitted against the brutal hostility of the policemen. The reader, who has participated in Geneviève's initiation into this women's world, now has no choice but to view the menace of enforced heterosexuality through the lesbians' defiant gaze, which turns back against their persecutors the shame and abjection the policemen had meant to provoke. Thus Blais is able to use the sympathetic perspective of her protagonist as a means of evoking her readers' sympathy for a more militant lesbian viewpoint.

Looking at Blais's book in the context of those by other Canadian women novelists, Coral Ann Howells suggests that Blais's image of a lesbian counterculture is linked to the quest for self-discovery of women and to the battle for identity of Quebec itself, and she finds a similar image of an underground culture in the work of the other major Quebec woman writer, Anne Hébert: "The 'underground' is intuitively right as the image of Quebec culture with its haunted sense of precarious survival."[4] Not just the expression of a particular group, in Howells's view, the struggles of the lesbian community in *Les Nuits de l'Underground* are linked to the multiple issues of marginality and oppression with which Blais's work has always been concerned: "Certainly for Blais there are strong connections between lesbian experience and larger historical patterns of oppression, so that by the end of *Nights in the Underground,* lesbianism begins to look like one particular example of marginality and idealism continually under threat from a barrage of hostile forces" (Howells, 160).

As the feminine solidarity Blais portrays offers the possibility of subverting society's hostile gaze, the women feel free to emerge from their subterranean existence. The later scenes of the novel become almost an allegory of the lesbian liberation of the 1970s in Quebec. The site of the women's gathering moves from the Underground bar to a restaurant opened by two members of the group, symbolically located on the second floor of an old house and explicitly designed to replace the darkness of the Underground with the light of day. The restaurant integrates non-lesbian women into the group, and it is connected with a theater, where all the women can participate in their friend Léa's dramatic representations of women's lives (in monologues that seem to echo those of *La Nef des sorcières*).

As the spring progresses the student Louise and her friends even dare to move beyond the safety of the traditional lesbian haunts, renovating several abandoned houses in a small rural community. They create a new lesbian space of their own and, in the process, force the other villagers to take them into account. It is into this renewed springtime world that Françoise will come to rejoin Geneviève after her return to health, which is fittingly termed a "resurrection." In contrast to the ambiguous springtime that closes *Une saison dans la vie d'Emmanuel,* the spring of *Les Nuits de l'Underground* seems to offer real reasons for hope, and the novel ends with a return to life made possible by the solidaristic love it has sought to portray. Although all is not yet perfect, the closing scenes of the novel are closer to a utopian vision than anything else in Blais's work.

As Gilles Marcotte points out, *Les Nuits de l'Underground* enables its readers to enter an unfamiliar milieu—the nighttime world of lesbian bars.[5] Yet if Blais describes the uniqueness of this world, with its varied characters and activities, she also insists it is grounded in the familiar reality of human relationships. It is in this spirit that Blais had hoped her novel would be received: "Je veux qu'on aborde ce livre comme un livre ordinaire. . . . La femme lesbienne n'est pas singulière, sinon dans l'esprit des gens [I want people to approach this book like any other. . . . The lesbian woman is not a being apart, except in people's minds]" (quoted in Roy, 33). If there is a "difference" in lesbian relationships, in Geneviève's view this difference is grounded simply in women's greater potential for caring and mutual comprehension. Although Blais does not minimize the importance of physical desire, her emphasis is on the many supportive relationships that unite the women, the numerous episodes in which they all come to the aid of a suffering sister.

As in many of Blais's works, the essence of this reality is summed up in a work of art: here, Rodin's sculpture of a mother holding her dying daughter. This sculpture represents for Geneviève "une maternité morale qu'elle avait souvent eu l'occasion d'observer entre femmes" ["the several different faces of maternity she'd often seen in women"] (46; 29). In reply to her male lover, who sees in her attraction to women only the effect of sexual desire, Geneviève affirms that relationships between women are, rather, a response to the unbearable anguish of human solitude: "un espoir, beaucoup plus secret, de guérir à deux ce que l'on ne peut soigner seule: une angoisse de vivre" ["It could help them cure as a couple what each was helpless to treat alone: an anguish in the face of life"] (46; 29). If Geneviève fails in her effort to deliver Lali from her solitary suffering, she is able to help Françoise, just as the combined care of Lali and Louise reanimates René, and the "amour solidaire" of the group warms their sick friend in the cold of the Quebec winter.

The concept of a network of women linked by mutual caring is both the subject and the dominant structural principle of *Les Nuits de l'Underground,* but Blais has only begun to realize its potential for reorienting her narrative. Her long, flowing sentences testify to the need for connection, the importance of establishing relationships, as they had in the work of Marcel Proust, whose influence is evident in the text. Blais had read Proust almost obsessively during her years in Wellfleet, as documented by her Notebooks, but Proustian tendencies appear most visibly in her work only a decade later. Blais's emphasis on multiple relationships, however, is not carried over into the narrative point of view, which is generally limited to Geneviève or a sympathetic third-person narrator. Geneviève's perspective functions effectively in allowing the reader to enter this strange new world along with her, as she rediscovers life in Quebec. But, as reviewers have noted, the emphasis on Geneviève diminishes the force of the novel, since as a character she lacks the interest and depth of figures like Lali or René. In her later novel, *Le Sourd dans la ville,* Blais was able to develop a narrative strategy that more accurately reflects the human network she was trying to develop on the thematic level.

L'Ange de la solitude

The fluid technique of shifting point of view is used effectively in Blais's second novel of lesbian community, *L'Ange de la solitude,* published in 1989. Here, as in *Les Nuits de l'Underground,* Blais creates a collective protagonist, a group of lesbian women. But in the 10 years that separate the two novels, her tone has become less militant and her outlook less optimistic. The group at the center of the novel is made up of young women known only by their private nicknames—L'Abeille (The Bee), Johnie, Gérard, Polydor, and Doudouline. They are a generation younger than the characters of *Les Nuits de l'Underground,* and the battles for gay and lesbian rights fought by their predecessors have apparently been won. These women live comfortably together in the house of L'Abeille, and their life-style does not seem to be an issue for themselves or for their mothers, who willingly sew their masculine clothing and invite them to share their summer homes.

Yet something continues to threaten their apparently peaceful existence. This threat leads them to gather together to protect the intimate reality of their lives, signaled by their use of private names that have meaning only within the group. Johnie becomes conscious of this new danger as she recoils from the contemptuous use of the term "lesbian" by her former lover, Marianne. Although she had planned to write an essay on the positive effects of linguistic transformation, on the joyous affirmation of the term *gay,* Johnie realizes that the long-awaited "Gay Era" is fast becoming what she calls the "Era of the Pink Star." A symbol that links the star worn by Jewish victims of the Holocaust with the pink triangle assigned to homosexuals, the "pink star" is used by Blais as a sign of the condemnation now borne within the bodies of a new oppressed race, the victims of AIDS.[6]

In the final scene where Gérard's ashes are scattered over the St. Lawrence, the young woman is tellingly identified with the AIDS victims of San Francisco, although her death is the result of fire rather than disease. For Johnie, AIDS has nullified the gains made by the gay liberation movement, becoming a weapon in the hands of church and state to use against the homosexual community. She now sees her own situation as a lesbian in a pessimistic light: "Echouée parmi ses contemporains de l'Etoile Rose, sa conquête d'une libération à vie comme sa frêle conquête de la vie, n'avaient jamais été aussi menacées [Thrown in with her contemporaries of the Pink Star, her conquest of a lifelong liberation, like her fragile conquest of life, had never been so threatened]."[7]

Johnie's black vision seems in many ways to echo Blais's. This is clear in the very structure of the novel, especially in its use of the seasonal cycle. In the late 1970s, the heyday of gay liberation, *Les Nuits de l'Underground* had used the seasons to underline its militant optimism, beginning in the cold of winter and ending in a promise-filled spring. In stark contrast, the commune of *L'Ange de la solitude* struggles through the heat of an oppressive summer only to end up facing a cold, gray November.

But although AIDS provides a menacing backdrop to their lives, the women's immediate problems are still the difficulties of the couple, the anguish of solitude. If these problems are at times alleviated by the solidarity of the group, the network of mutual caring does not provide the solution it had seemed to offer in *Les Nuits de l'Underground*. L'Abeille abandons the security of a house filled with friends to indulge her violent desire with men she picks up on the street, and Johnie leads a hidden private life with Lynda, a shopgirl she maintains as a mistress. When Lynda abandons her, Johnie flees to a tropical island rather than seeking the support of her friends. Johnie's flight is not without consequences: in her absence, Gérard wanders off into a world of drugs and alcohol, where she eventually dies in a tenement fire. In this supposedly solidaristic group, only the voluptuous Doudouline and her devoted Polydor seem to find happiness with each other, but even their happiness is marred by its inattentiveness to the needs of others.

In *Les Nuits de l'Underground* Blais had offered art as a counterbalance to the weight of human solitude. Geneviéve had transmuted her pain into sculpture, and Léa's theater was able to speak the unspoken reality of women's lives. In *L'Ange de la solitude* all the women are artists, which would seem to imply an even stronger assertion of the saving powers of art. But this does not prove to be the case: with the possible exception of the singer Doudouline and her actress mother, these lesbian artists are repeatedly shown as blocked in their creative efforts. The older painter Paula, a successful set designer, hides away her most personal work, testimony to her secret despair. L'Abeille completes a painting of her lover, Thérèse, but when their relationship comes to an end she finds it difficult to find new inspiration.

The most noticeable failure is that of Johnie, the writer who has taken her name from Radclyffe Hall as she seeks to emulate her predecessor's daring work. In *Les Nuits de l'Underground* Geneviève's emotional pain had provided material for her work: in sharp contrast, when Johnie is abandoned by Lynda, she finds herself unable to write. She is working on an essay, presumably on lesbian writing, entitled "From Sappho to Radclyffe Hall," but she actually produces very little. Perhaps, suggests L'Abeille, Johnie should be writing on something more closely related to her own experience—the present reality of the commune. (Of course, the reader cannot fail to remark that this is the subject Blais has chosen for her own study of the lesbian condition.) But Johnie seems unable to transform her life into art: "Elle prodiguait ailleurs que dans l'écriture la manne inépuisable de son expérience [She distributed the inexhaustible manna of her experience to things other than her writing]" (26). Her life is marked by the repeated promise to "write about this tomorrow," but she never realizes her creative aspirations.

Although Blais does not directly relate it to their inability to create, these young women share something of the sensitivity of Anna in *Visions d'Anna:* they are conscious of living their lives against the background of the poverty and violence of the contemporary world. Johnie is shocked by her lover's indifference to the fate of the Palestinians, Doudouline writes songs about her memories of Haiti, Thérèse leaves L'Abeille to devote herself to the homeless. At one point the idealistic Thérèse imagines an entire network of women, linked by car phones, who would care for teenage runaways. But Thérèse's expanded vision of caring is not a dominant one in this novel; in fact, her friends reject her moralizing tendencies and refuse to sacrifice their independence to join her new commune.

Despite the noticeable tempering of Blais's optimism, however, *L'Ange de la solitude* still seeks to affirm the value of group solidarity that had animated *Les Nuits de l'Underground.* It also reaffirms the positive vision of the mother-daughter relationship at the center of *Visions d'Anna.* In *L'Ange de la solitude* the mother-daughter couple is constituted by the singer Doudouline and her hippie-turned-actress mother, Sophie. Using a fluid narrative technique of shifting point of view, Blais views this complex but loving relationship from the perspective of both mother and daughter, recording Doudouline's irritation with her mother's efforts to run her life and Sophie's impatience with her daughter's lack of direction, in combination with her unending demands. Yet the mother is always there to respond to the daughter's needs, and, as the novel approaches its end, it is the collaboration of mother and daughter that makes possible Doudouline's successful debut in a concert where she performs her own work—a performance that commands the admiration even of Doudouline's ephemeral "fathers." This triumph is a tribute to the mother-daughter relationship that, Blais implies, will continue to provide a grounding for Doudouline's creative work.

The supportive mother-daughter relationship is linked to the lesbian commune as Sophie assumes, in a sense, the role of mother to them all when she leads them in a ritual dispersal of Gérard's ashes. If the network of feminine caring has failed to solve the personal problems of L'Abeille and Johnie, the alternative of solitary existence appears to offer even less. A model of complete autonomy is provided in the older artist, Paula, and her rejection of the ethic of group solidarity is made clear by her enraged reaction to L'Abeille when she attempts to renew her contacts with the group. Yet Paula's aura of happy self-sufficiency is put in doubt by L'Abeille's discovery of the hidden etchings that bear witness to her secret despair. And the very possibility of self-sufficiency is laid open to question when, in a symbolic act, Paula stubbornly insists on swimming against a rip tide on an isolated Mexican beach. Her pride receives a devastating blow when she must be rescued by a man, a foreigner who does not—as she significantly remarks—speak her language.

If even the strong cannot survive alone, more fragile beings like Gérard are lost when they wander away from the protection of the group. If the group is unable to provide emotional sustenance to all its members, if its mutual caring is less than perfect, it still provides the only possible alternative to the inhuman realm of solitude to which the title refers.

The title, however, reflects the ambiguity that permeates the entire novel. This "angel of solitude" is another in the company of angels who have defined Blais's literary vision, from Dürer's Angel of *Manuscrits de Pauline Archange* and Pauline Archange herself to the angelic Judith Lange of *Le Sourd dans la ville*. The angel of solitude, as described in the quotation from Jean Genet that serves as the novel's epigraph, presents a far less sympathetic figure than its predecessors. As defined by Genet, the angel of solitude, "more and more inhuman," is surrounded by music devoid of harmony—he is, in fact, "what remains when harmony is absent." The inhumanity, the absence of harmony with which the "angel of solitude" is associated, makes him a negative, even frightening figure. And, as we know from Blais's public statements, harmony occupies an important place in her hierarchy of values. When asked by Myrna Delson-Karan in April 1988, not long before the novel's publication, to sum up in one word what is most important to her, Blais answered almost immediately, "Harmony."[8]

Later on in the novel, however, Blais's angel of solitude assumes heroic proportions as Johnie hears him urging her to abandon the comforting but illusory camouflage of the group to assert herself against the world, presumably in defense of lesbian rights: "Quand donc défendras-tu tes droits? Toi qui es un soldat sans armes, quand donc cesseras-tu de te camoufler dans le feuillage qui t'abrite chez les filles de la bande, quand donc seras-tu toi-même, face au monde, dans une clarté resplendissante? [When are you going to stand up for your rights? You who are an unarmed soldier, when are you going to stop hiding in the sheltering foliage with the girls of the group, when are you going to be yourself in brilliant splendor before the world?]" (109). If solitude is an essential element of courageous action, it seems also to be, as Gérard laments, a necessary condition of Johnie's writing. If Blais's vision of solidarity is more nuanced in *L'Ange de la solitude,* so, too, is her understanding of the role of solitude. Never given to facile solutions, Blais, in her later work, has intensified her sensitivity to the ambiguity of the human condition.

Chapter Ten

A Community of Suffering: *Le Sourd dans la ville*

Published a full 20 years after Blais's first novel, *Le Sourd dans la ville (Deaf to the City)* reveals her continuing preoccupation with the problems of human solitude, the difficulties of communication, and the impossibility of love. *La Belle Bête* told the story of a lonely woman, unloved by her mother and abandoned by her husband, who is finally driven to suicide. This is also the fate of Florence, the central character of *Le Sourd dans la ville,* who is as alone and abandoned as the young Isabelle-Marie. Blais's fundamental vision of the human condition has not changed, but in *Le Sourd dans la ville* she seems to find a human force capable of combating this cruel and tragic reality. Through the very structure of her narrative she begins to re-create a community within which her solitary beings can find their place, and she envisions new models of human relationships to replace the outmoded traditional structures of family and Church, whose concepts and images she nevertheless reclaims.

Most important, in this novel Blais finds a narrative voice capable of expressing her new vision of human reality, and this accounts for the importance of *Le Sourd dans la ville* in Blais's artistic evolution. This narrative voice, which might more properly be termed a narrative consciousness, is capable of representing at the same time the solitude and the solidarity of human beings, and the workings of this narrative consciousness itself displaces characters and events to provide the action of the novel. As had not been the case in earlier novels, writing itself becomes an object of reflection, and Florence's meditations on her new perception of the world offers a mise-en-abyme of Blais's own narrative strategies.

The novel is populated by a disparate cast of characters who wander through an unidentified city that resembles Montreal, gathering from time to time in the bar of the seedy Hotel des Voyageurs. The hotel is run by the warm-hearted Gloria, who divides her time between her clients, her children, and her job as a strip-tease artist. For her son Mike, who is slowly dying of a brain tumor, she constructs the beautiful dream of a motorcycle trip through the American West, but it is clear this trip will never take place, that Mike will live out his short life caring for his little sister and helping out with the hotel. Gloria has a special affection for the homeless Irishman Tim, despondent over the necessity of parting with his beloved dog in order to enter an old-age home. A newly arrived guest is the middle-aged Florence, bent on ending her unhappy life, but who, along with the hotel's other denizens, looks forward to the visit of the young philosophy professor Judith Lange, who, as her name suggests, is an angel of mercy. This world of suffering and dying people is held together by the loving presence of Gloria and Judith and by the narrative consciousness, which moves effortlessly from one character to another.

Blais's previous novels, especially *Une saison dans la vie d'Emmanuel,* had participated in the critique of the religious tradition and the wave of secularization that had swept over Quebec in the 1960s. If God is absent from the contemporary universe of *Le Sourd dans la ville,* Blais gives us another creative force in the character of Gloria, mother of many children and maternal presence for the lost souls who frequent her bar. Her Hotel des Voyageurs is, in a sense, the world in microcosm, and it is significant that it is run by a woman, Gloria, whose name evokes the rest of the phrase: "in excelsis deo." In the text she calls herself "eternal Gloria, celestial Gloria."[1] Gloria's role seems quite natural for a woman, more natural than the sculptures of the Chartres cathedral, where Judith registers surprise that the life-giving role has been attributed to a man.

What has always been the norm in the Judaeo-Christian vision of the world becomes, in Judith's eyes, an aberration. Blais's feminine deity is associated with water, the maternal element, and the flow of milk:

> Elle qui donnait le biberon, à tous les hommes, aucune philosophie ne pouvait être au dessus de celle que Gloria dispensait à tous en baignant des fluides de son corps l'aridité de cette terre où tout ce que l'on aimait allait mourir demain. [She gave all men their bottle, there could be no higher philosophy than the one Gloria dispensed to all, her body's fluids drenching the arid earth where everything one loved would die tomorrow.] (18; 12)

In contrast to God the Father, who has offered himself to human sinners by having his son born of a woman, Gloria chooses the most criminal of men as fathers of her children.

If Gloria plays the role of God the Mother in Blais's new Trinity, her son Mike is her "crucified one." In his suffering and his expectation of an early death, Mike plays the Christ-like role of sacrificial lamb, which is also signaled by his name, Michel Agneli. He appears to Florence as Jesus as he comes toward her to offer her a plate of burned spaghetti:

> Sur les vomissures du tapis marchait cet être comme Jésus sur des eaux boueuses, Jésus dont elle n'avait jamais aimé l'histoire, car il n'existait pas et celui qui venait vers elle existait, c'était sans doute lui, le fils de Gloria. [He was walking over vomit stains on the rug like Jesus on the muddy waters, Jesus whose story she'd never liked for he didn't exist, while the human being who was coming towards her did, Gloria's son surely.] (64; 62)

Florence's criticism of the traditional figure of Jesus is revealing: in her eyes he simply fails to exist. In the place of a religion based on abstract and fictional beings, Blais proposes a trinity of completely human values: the maternal love of Gloria, the innocent suffering of Mike, and, in the place of the Holy Ghost, the inflamed conscience of Judith Langenais, a name symbolically shortened into Judith Lange (Judith the Angel).

Just as Gloria is completely involved in the creation of physical life, Judith devotes herself to the life of the spirit, in her profession as a philosopher. If Gloria is associated with water, the maternal element, Judith is associated with fire, recalling the biblical tongues of fire used to represent the presence of the Holy Spirit. The arrival of Judith Lange is impatiently awaited by both Mike and Florence, but, like the Holy Spirit, Judith is slow to "descend" to them (from the heights where she lives and works) after a first appearance toward the beginning of the novel. Although she has very little contact with the other characters, she has a magnetic and transforming effect on them, and it is especially through the reflections of others that she has a strong presence in the text—a presence more spiritual than physical.

If she is a new representation of the Creator, Gloria also offers a new vision of the mother. In many ways she is a caricature of all the pious traditional images of the Quebec mother with her many children. With her dying son, her rebellious older daughter, her tireless service to her children, Gloria echoes the idealized mother depicted by Gabrielle Roy in her classic novel of Montreal, *Bonheur d'occasion (The Tin Flute)*. It is through the figure of Gloria that *Le Sourd dans la ville* signals its inscription in the Quebec literary tradition. But Blais radically alters the traditionally sexless maternal stereotype as Gloria opens her heart—and her bed—to all men and practices the profession of strip-tease in a nightclub called the Infinity of Sex.

Gloria's profession creates a rather amusing disjunction with the traditional image, but this is not only a humorous note: it is also Blais's reintegration in the maternal of woman's sexual nature, so long repressed by the ideal of the virgin mother. It was, after all, a rejection of sexuality that constituted the repressive side of Grand-Mère Antoinette in *Une saison dans la vie d'Emmanuel*. But after creating numerous portraits of cold and distant mothers and repressive grandmothers, Blais finally offers a positive vision of a woman who is a mother—and with it the possibility of the renewal of the family as a form of human community. And Gloria's family is not limited to her own children: she welcomes all those who come to her hotel. In this way her role is similar to that of the celibate Judith Lange, who also plays a maternal role for the solitary and tormented beings to whom she constantly ministers.

If all the characters in *Le Sourd dans la ville* are linked by their association with Gloria and Judith, they are linked in a much deeper way by their inscription in a narrative that, by its very form, indicates their participation in a human community. The narrative voice is capable of entering into the thoughts of each character, even the cat who wanders the streets. But unlike many modern multivoiced narratives that juxtapose divergent perspectives, Blais's narrative voice underlines the common experience of the human condition—one that, for Blais as for Pascal, is determined by death, suffering, and solitude. Sometimes the experience of one character is explicitly linked to that of another—"Tim l'Irlandais et son chien pouvaient tout aussi bien s'appeler Florence car ils étaient comme elle, soumis à la violence des bourreaux suprêmes" ["Tim the Irishman and his dog might just as well be called Florence for they were, like her, subjected to the violence of the supreme tormentors"] (50; 47)—but much more powerful links are forged by the narrative voice as it passes from the consciousness of one character to another without pausing.

Very often the passage from one character to another is effected in the text by a simple linking, by the elementary mechanism of a comma and the conjunction "and":

> Cette humble offrande . . . qui était si peu entre Florence et son mari, pensait-elle, et que longtemps avait été l'emblème de ses raisons de vivre de la stabilité de son coeur, de son esprit, et Berthe Agnela pensait, qu'y a-t-il de l'autre côté de la montagne mauve. [The humble offering that . . . had been such a small thing between Florence and her husband, she thought, and yet it had been the emblem of her reason to live, of the sta-

bility of her heart, of her spirit, for a long time; and Berthe Agneli asked herself what was on the other side of the purple mountain.] (116–17; 117–18)

The narrative voice never fails to name the character in question, and the narrative is sprinkled with indications (as here, "pensait-elle," "et Berthe Agneli pensait") of point of view. For Blais, this form of multivoiced interior monologue is not a literary game whose object is to mystify the reader but a way of expressing a certain human reality.

At times, as the narrative consciousness passes from one character to another, there is a fragment of sentence that could just as easily belong to either one. As the perspective passes from the thoughts of Judith's mother to the experience of Mike, the thought that the city would soon be filled with sweet-smelling flowers may belong to either character or be shared by both: "Judith avait un souffle chaud, la ville serait bientôt toute fleurie, odorante, et pendant que sa soeur jouait à ses pieds, Mike s'était légèrement assoupi, debout contre l'arbre" ["Judith's breath was hot, before long the whole city would be in blossom, fragrant, so fragrant, and Mike had dozed off vaguely while his sister played at his feet, he was still standing against the tree"] (21; 16). The transition element could be, as here, a common experience of spring, a bit of dialogue heard by several characters at once, or an act they are all in a position to see. And sometimes it is a series of parallel thoughts, which unite two characters who are physically at a distance.

The almost imperceptible transitions between different minds function to stress the shared elements of human experience rather than the differences. This is not to say that the experience of all the characters in the novel constitutes an undifferentiated whole: from time to time there is the brusque halt at the end of the sentence and a new beginning with another character in a distant place. But this is rather the exception than the rule.

Unlike most authors who use a limited point of view, Blais does not always find it necessary to submit the narrative voice to the strict limits of a character's vision. The narrative consciousness is capable of seeing people and events from outside as well as inside, capable of registering acts and words spoken aloud as well as the hidden thoughts and memories of a single character. Florence, for example, can be for the reader a gray shape, seen from outside, or, from her own perspective, a wondering vision of an abandoned world. All these perspectives and experiences enter into the weaving of the apparently homogeneous thread of the narration—a homogeneity resulting from the invariable use of third-person pronouns and the imperfect tense.

Although Blais often uses stream-of-consciousness narration, she refuses to observe the strict limits generally associated with this technique. Blais's narrative voice is capable of expressing certain aspects of the interior life of characters of which they are not themselves aware. Florence is often a vehicle for this type of narrative expansion: she is endowed with the ability to sense and articulate in others feelings of which they themselves are only dimly conscious.

The perspective of Florence seems to mirror the functioning of the narrative consciousness, and her reflections often expose and describe Blais's narrative strategies. When Florence is suddenly deprived of her husband's love, which had dominated her emotional life—and had thus, metaphorically, rendered her blind and deaf to others—she suddenly becomes extraordinarily aware of all that surrounds her. She becomes, as she says, "transparent": "Ses mains, ses yeux, son corps ne la défendaient plus contre cette transparence du froid, tout en elle résonnait de cette froideur, de cette solitude, le malheur des autres" ["Her hands, her eyes, her body no longer defended her against this transparency of the cold, her entire being was vibrant with this coldness, this solitude, with other people's misfortunes"] (53; 50).

Florence's acutely sensitive perspective dominates the novel: she occupies a central position, as privileged observer of most of the characters, and passages narrated from her point of view take up the greatest number of pages. Florence's vision of events is the one director Mireille Dansereau ended by choosing, with good reason, as the central focus of her film adaptation of the novel. It would even be possible to speculate that the narrative consciousness is, in fact, really that of Florence and that all the other characters only exist in her imagination or her intuition of their thoughts. But that would be to limit the vision of the novel, which resists restricting itself to the reality of a single character. Rather, Florence's understanding vision—and her meditation on it—can be seen as a sort of mise-en-abyme of the functioning of the author's more comprehensive narrative voice.

If the functioning of the narrative consciousness is revealed through the character of Florence, its extreme sensitivity to human suffering and solitude is incarnated in the character of Judith Lange. For Blais and her characters, to attain this consciousness of suffering is to combat the limits of the human condition—limits always characterized by the adjec-

tives "blind" and "deaf." Blindness and deafness are repeatedly equated
with death: "La mort venait vers vous, aveugle et sourde, . . . sous
l'aspect d'un bourreau aveugle et sourd" ["Death closed in like something blind and deaf, sometimes it even came at the hands of a blind,
deaf executioner"] (37; 33). Most human beings live as Florence had
lived in her previous life, indifferent to all that is not their own existence,
or like Berthe Agneli, who tries to isolate herself from a human reality
too painful to bear: "Je suis sourde à tout" ["I'm deaf to everything"]
(145; 149), she declares.

If it is through the model of Florence's recently awakened consciousness that we are opened to the suffering beings who surround us, it is
through the consciousness of Judith Lange that we understand the reality of suffering throughout history:

> Les paroles de Judith Lange résonnant dans la gare déserte, . . . on ne
> peut rien oublier, les pyramides d'Egypte, les temples grecs, on les con-
> templait placidement car le silence des siècles avait enseveli la voix des
> esclaves mais le cri de la torture s'échappait encore parfois de ces lèvres
> scellées par un éternel secret, mais nous étions si sourds que nous l'enten-
> dions à peine. [The memory of Judith Lange's words resounded in the
> deserted train station: . . . you cannot forget anything, you could placidly
> contemplate Egyptian pyramids and Greek temples for the silence of cen-
> turies had engulfed the voices of the slaves, and yet from time to time a
> cry of torture still escaped from those lips sealed by an eternal secret only
> we were so deaf we barely perceived it.] (172; 177)

It is Judith's message that we are all united in a suffering to which we
must not attempt to blind ourselves—a message, as I have pointed out,
expressed in the novel's narrative form.

According to the numerous discussions of art and music in the text,
the communication of this message, the awakening of this consciousness,
has already been the objective of great works of art—those, for example,
of Toulouse-Lautrec, whose aim is to penetrate the indifference of the
spectator:

> Il avait rapproché du monde visible, de notre indifférence, ce que nous
> tenions à oublier, ces visages, ces destins, ces existences dont il avait tenté
> de comprendre le secret. [All these things we prefer to forget—these
> faces, these destinies, these lives whose secrets and enigma the artist had
> tried to understand—came dangerously close to the visible world, to our
> indifference.] (106; 107)

If the recognition of the tragic truth of the human condition can be terrifying, in rather paradoxical fashion it can also be the source of a great hope, as in the last work of Mozart, where the terror of approaching death is counterbalanced by the appreciation of the grace of life:

> Cette Messe, pensait Florence, Mozart l'a peut-être écrite lorsqu'il a aperçu la grâce de la vie pour la dernière fois, . . . et cette musique lui fut inspirée, non comme un chant de résignation mais un orgueilleux appel à l'espoir. [Perhaps Mozart felt the grace of life for the last time when he composed that mass, thought Florence, . . . perhaps he'd been inspired to write that music, not as a song of resignation but as a proud call to hope.] (172; 177)

Such sensitivity to human suffering is not, for Blais, a source of pessimism.

As in the last work of Mozart, where Florence finds "a proud call to hope," there is in *Le Sourd dans la ville* an element of hope that was noticeably absent from Blais's early novels. This hope is linked to an affirmation of human values that, like the literary form in which they are inscribed, are strongly marked by the feminine. The universe of the novel is not a hierarchy or linear progression but a network of beings linked by profound and multiple relationships. The very structure of *Le Sourd dans la ville* thus reproduces that "web of interconnection" that moral theorist Carol Gilligan has proposed as the image most accurately expressing the concept of moral responsibility articulated by women.[2] There is not a single protagonist who affirms himself over or against the others but several central characters, whose importance is the consequence of their intense sensitivity to those around them.

The narrative voice, especially, refuses the limits imposed on linear literary narration by the concept of a unitary personality surrounded by impenetrable limits. On the contrary, Blais's narrative voice reveals the permeability of these limits, which also become apparent to the characters. This universe of permeable ego boundaries and interlocking relationships seems to echo the description of feminine personality proposed by sociologist Nancy Chodorow. For Chodorow, feminine personality is characterized by "flexible and permeable ego boundaries": "the basic feminine sense of self is connected to the world" (Chodorow, 106). Chodorow's terminology could very well be applied to the characters, and especially to the narrative voice, in *Le Sourd dans la ville*. Thus the vision of a human community founded on comprehension and empathy that Blais creates in *Le Sourd dans la ville* can be seen as an expansion to a wider sphere of the women's network of caring in *Les Nuits de l'Underground*. As in the earlier novel, Blais has here given form to a vision that, in the terms suggested by Chodorow and Gilligan, is profoundly marked by the feminine.

Chapter Eleven
Coming Home: *Visions d'Anna*

Visions d'Anna, ou le vertige (Anna's World) reflects Blais's continuing pre-occupation with the precarious state of the world, but her characteristically dark vision is lightened by a tempered optimism, especially evident in her portrayal of relationships among women. In fact, in the context of Blais's entire work, *Visions d'Anna* offers one of the most positive expressions of the possibilities for human life. While *Le Sourd dans la ville* is not without its hopeful side, despite the depressing events of the plot, this hope is much more evident—and more clearly articulated—in *Visions d'Anna.* There is an evident continuity between the two novels: a continuity of style and, particularly, a continuity of vision. *Le Sourd dans la ville* and *Visions d'Anna* could be seen as forming a cycle, in which the problems posed in the first are, in some way, resolved in the second.

Very evident as a link between the two novels is the structure of the journey, of departure and return, which seems to dominate the action. At the end of *Le Sourd dans la ville* appear the words of Judith Lange, who pleads vainly with Florence to come back to life. But in this novel the appeal to ties to humanity and life on the earth comes too late. Florence has just killed herself and even the great tenderness of Judith Lange cannot bring her back to life, no more than Gloria's maternal love, as admirable as it is, can save her dying son.

In *Visions d'Anna,* however, Judith's appeal is repeated, in the same words ("come back, come back"), and these words are finally heeded: the journey back is completed, and the wanderers return to the maternal home. In contrast to the futile appeal of Judith that closes *Le Sourd dans la ville, Visions d'Anna* ends on the hopeful voice of Anna's mother, who confirms the reality of Anna's return to life: "Je pense que cette fois elle est de retour" ["I think this time she's come back"].[1]

The model of departure and return home is repeated in the three family groups—or, more exactly, the three groups formed by mothers and their children—around which the novel is structured. In the two more important of these families the central relationships are those of mothers and daughters—Anna and her mother, Raymonde, and Guislaine and her daughters Michelle and Liliane. The two families are closely linked together by ties of friendship and complicity: Raymonde and Guislaine are high school classmates, and Michelle would like to be Anna's friend, despite their difference in age. Both Michelle and Anna have run away from their mothers into a despairing world of drifters and drug addicts. Anna undertakes a real journey by going to the Caribbean to live with the "drifters," but even after her return to Montreal she remains separated from the others in the isolated island of her room, contemplating her private visions. After getting arrested in a drug raid, Michelle, too, seems to come back to reality and manages to reestablish communication with her mother.

A third family seems to repeat the same scenario in a less affluent milieu—one approaching absolute destitution. The nameless woman from the mining town of Asbestos, abandoned without resources by her alcoholic husband, has moved in with a new lover as she struggles to make a life for her children. But the man's brutality causes her young son to run away from home, and she must go out to find him, to bring him back. The image of this mother, who wanders through the fog looking for a child repelled by the violence and indifference of men, establishes a schematic model of the much more nuanced drama of the other two families.

Even more than in *Le Sourd dans la ville,* most of the words in the novel, although they belong to the characters, are not spoken aloud. These interior monologues do not become speech but remain just beneath the level of verbal expression in a flow of subterranean words that resembles the *sous-conversations* of Nathalie Sarraute. The presence of unspoken words is made explicit in a description of Anna: "Les mots hésitaient à ses lèvres mais elle les entendait qui frappaient violemment la cage de son crâne" ["The words faltered on her lips but she could hear them pounding against the cage of her skull"] (62; 49). As in Sarraute, there is a contrast between the *conversations,* the dialogue spoken aloud by the characters (indicated by quotation marks in the text), generally by the adults of the novel, and the *sous-conversation,* the unspoken words of the children. This difference is not far from reproducing the distinction established by Julia Kristeva between the symbolic order, "the order of verbal communication, the paternal order of descent",[2] and the non-verbal semiotic, which belongs to the maternal, the feminine.

The words spoken by the adults—and the adults are the only ones to speak in the beginning of the novel—seem to precipitate the flight of the children. Anna takes refuge in the silence of her room, far from the voices of her mother and her friends, and Michelle isolates herself in a world of music to efface her parents' constant judgments. In the first and the last scenes of the novel Anna is listening to the conversation of her mother's friends, in which she does not participate. For her this conversation is meaningless: "Elle semblait demander à sa mère, mais quel est donc votre but, pourquoi vous acharnez-vous ainsi, à tout expliquer, tout dire" ["Her intense grey gaze seemed to be asking her mother, what do you really want, why do you try so desperately to explain everything, to say everything"] (11; 3). The adults talk of the future, but, for Anna, this future has become uncertain because of the threats of destruction that hover over the earth; she wonders, "Savaient-ils que leurs paroles étaient usées jusqu'à la lie" ["Did they know their words were threadbare"]? (11; 3). In response Anna has chosen to take refuge in a mute, reclusive existence.

The words before which Anna tries to flee are especially those of her father, Peter, whose voice she had always perceived as a hostile force: "Peter pénétrait de sa voix impérative l'univers d'Anna" ["He and his imperious voice would enter Anna's world"] (163; 138). Peter is the father who possesses the power to name things and thus to affirm his ownership, as he writes the name of his new little daughter on the bracelet he puts on her wrist, "le bracelet d'or qui la tiendrait demain captive de ses illusions, de sa conquête du monde" ["the gold bracelet that, tomorrow would hold her captive to his illusions, his conquest of the world"] (94; 77). For Peter, language is used to dominate, to signify possession: he says, "Voici ma nouvelle petite fille, ma nouvelle maison, ma nouvelle piscine" ["Here's my new little girl, my new house, my new swimming pool"] (95; 77). But this power of indicating possession implies the related power of delimiting, excluding, forbidding. After naming his domain, Peter excludes his daughter from it: "Je ne veux pas vous voir ici, dans ma maison, dans ma piscine, auprès de ma femme, de mon enfant" ["I don't want you here in my house, in my pool, around my wife and child"] (95; 77). His words incarnate the symbolic order, as defined by Kristeva—an order of human symbolism that operates by prohibition and division.

Peter's speech to his daughter is nothing but a flood of interdictions: "enlever [t]a bicyclette de là" ["move your bicycle"] (43; 32); "Pense à l'avenir . . . redresse-toi" ["Think of the future . . . straighten up"] (44; 32); "Ne touche pas à tout, forbidden" ["Don't touch everything, you mustn't"] (44; 33). Turning his back on his past as a conscientious objector to the Vietnam War, Peter now lives in the symbolic order, "dans l'application des lois" ["within the law"] (51; 38). He is thus capable of designating those who should be excluded from the social system, using the English words *drifters* and *runaway children,* seeing in them the debris of another world. As he has refused to recognize his daughter when she was out with her friends, he grants himself the right to forbid her access to his house, which represents for Anna the whole social structure. Perhaps Peter, as Blais says, "n'était peut-être qu'un père, comme tant d'autres de sa génération" ["was just a father like so many others of his generation"] (114; 94), but he represents a system of masculine authority that Anna's mother recognizes as the one she has to fight every day, at the Correctional Institute, at the Juvenile Court. The house of the father, sustained by the educational system and the law, becomes a prison that condemns all difference.

The discourse of Michelle's parents is parallel to Peter's. It is her parents' voices that she tries to escape with her drug addict friends: "ces mots, ces phrases qui la hantaient, ce qu'ils disaient, ce qu'ils ne disaient pas, pourquoi la harcelaient-ils, sous le martèlement de ces voix, elle pliait en deux" ["the words, the phrases that haunted her, what they said, what they didn't say, why were they pestering her, as she walked she bent double under the pounding of their voices"] (104; 86). For Michelle, too, the voice of her father, Paul, a sociology professor, seems to drive her from his life: "son père qui savait parler de tout, échauffé par ses certitudes et le son de sa propre voix grave" ["her father, who could talk about everything, excited by his certainties and the sound of his own solemn voice"] (125; 104). Like Anna's father, Paul is ready to define the reactions of his two daughters in terms of abnormality and sickness. Without even trying to understand Michelle's excessive sensitivity, he decides she is "a case for the psychiatrist," thereby sparing himself the necessity of understanding her. Thus, when Michelle tries to express herself to her parents by telling them about her dreams, her father tells her to save it for her analyst: "Il faut raconter tout cela au psychiatre qui te soigne, ta mère et moi, nous avons déjà bien assez de soucis à ton sujet" ["You must tell that to the psychiatrist looking after you, your mother and I are worried about you enough as it is"] (104; 85).

Although they retain some sympathy for their younger daughter, both parents agree in condemning the homosexuality of their older daughter, Liliane. The sociologist father feels he has the right to proclaim lesbians as cases of "deviant sexuality," and he would like to exclude this daughter from his family. He wants to tell Liliane, as she cares for Michelle, "Lesbienne . . . ne touche pas à notre fille" ["Lesbian, . . . keep your hands off our daughter"] (126; 105). In Liliane's case, her mother

shelters herself in her role of support for the symbolic order, identifying
with the authority of the father:

> Elle lui interdirait de vivre avec une amie dans sa maison, ce pouvoir était
> encore le sien, celui de Paul, leur secrète dictature, leur complicité, on
> pouvait encore leur dire "tant que vous serez sous notre toit, vous devrez
> nous obéir." [She would forbid her to live in her house with a girlfriend,
> she still had that power, and Paul, their secret dictatorship, their com-
> plicity, they could still say, "As long as you're under our roof you must
> obey us."] (130; 108)

When she is not dreaming of excluding Liliane, she repeats the gesture
of Anna's father by refusing to recognize her daughter's identity. Liliane
tries to understand this refusal as the result of her mother's jealousy:
Guislaine has made a career of putting others' needs before her own and
does not possess Liliane's ability to freely express her sensuality.

Although she shares her husband's judgment of Liliane, Guislaine
refuses to share his readiness to put a label on Michelle's problems. She
reacts against the definitions proposed by her husband by saying, "C'est
nous qui ne la comprenons pas, nous devrions simplement nous dire
qu'elle est unique, qu'on ne peut la comparer à personne d'autre"
["We're the ones who don't understand her, we should simply tell ourselves that she's unique, that she can't be compared to anyone else"]
(108; 88). Thus, like Raymonde, Guislaine refuses participation in the
imprisonment of the symbolic order, and it is by this refusal that the two
mothers succeed in maintaining a point of contact with their daughters.

If it is the paternal language that forces the daughters to close themselves off in a world of silence, Blais sees communication between
women as existing in this very silence, thus outside of the symbolic
order. There is Anna's dream, in which her mother and she do not speak
but seek each other's eyes. There is the moment of communication
between Michelle and Guislaine, where the mother's tears bring forth a
silent gesture from the daughter, who takes her mother in her arms.[3]
But even the communication between mother and daughter, which
recalls the preoedipal relationship that precedes access to speech, cannot
completely dispense with language. The fragile link between Anna and
her mother is maintained by a series of postcards signed with the single
word "Anna." And the moment of silent communication between
Michelle and Guislaine necessarily leads to a conversation in which each
one can finally express her understanding of the other's suffering. Anna's
silence is a way of refusing complicity in the crimes of men, but it also
means renouncing her ties with humanity. When she remains silent in

the face of Michelle's desperate appeal, Anna, for the first time, begins to criticize her own refusal of language: "Fallait-il rejeter la supplication de ce visage qu'un seul sourire, un seul mot eussent suffi à éclairer?" ["Must she reject the supplication on that face when just one smile, one word, would have been enough to light it up?"] (91; 74).

Liliane is the first person who is able to use language to reach Michelle. Halfway between language and a form of wordless communication, the conversation of Liliane and Michelle is characterized as "murmurs," and they are linked by a silent complicity. It is also through Liliane's vision that Blais begins to sketch out the possibility of using language not only to permit communication between victims but to combat the repression of the symbolic order. In response to the "treacherous words" of the chiefs of state, Liliane sees other words springing up everywhere—words that could be "fragile shields" against the destruction of the earth. Reappropriating the paternal power of naming and constituting a genealogy, her professor of sculpture, a woman, transmits to her the heroic names of woman like Rosa Luxemburg, women "qui avaient confronté les meurtres de l'Histoire" ["who had confronted the murders of History"] (198; 170). And Liliane begins to imagine a form of women's writing capable overcoming the imprisoning forces: "Autrefois des femmes avaient écrit en prison, nulle règle les avait asservies, elles avaient écrit, je vis, je résiste, je ne céderai pas" ["In the past women had written in prison, no rule had enslaved them, they had written, I am alive, I resist, I will not give in"] (199; 171).

Blais gives us no example of Liliane's own writing, if it is not *Visions d'Anna* itself, which seems to correspond in some measure to Liliane's desires. Marie Couillard suggests that, in a sort of mise-en-abyme, this book is already being written in Blais's text by Raymonde's erstwile lover, Alexandre, who makes his life with the marginal and the homeless, the "drifters" of contemporary society.[4] It is through his eyes that the reader has followed the wanderings of the woman from Asbestos.

The qualities of an ideal writing are suggested by Guislaine's negative reaction to the book she is reading: "morne agressivité dans ces mots structurés et froids" ["in the cold, structured words there was only dismal hostility"]. What Guislaine would prefer would be "l'intuition, la finesse répondant aux nostalgies de son coeur" ["the intuition, the acuity that would match her heart's nostalgia"] (107; 108), what could be called a feminine style of writing, an *écriture au féminin*. This is what Blais has already found in her own writing, in the fluid narrative voice of *Visions d'Anna,* which flows from one character to another, and in the images of an ideal world, expressed in dreams that seem to circulate among the women.

Chapter Twelve

Reflections on a Writer's Life:
Parcours d'un écrivain:
Notes américaines

The volume Blais published in 1993, *Parcours d'un écrivain: Notes améri-caines (A Writer's Journey: Notes from America)*, presents itself as a collection of disparate essays. As the author explains, the separate sections were written as weekly columns published in the literary pages of the Montreal daily paper *Le Devoir* over the course of a year.

The essays present themselves as reflections on the years she spent in the United States during the 1960s, in the university town of Cambridge, Massachusetts, and in the intellectual community of Wellfleet on Cape Cod. But her perspective is that of the early 1990s—a present shaped by her immersion in another, parallel group of writers and artists centered in Key West, Florida. Like Wellfleet, Key West is a community determined less by geography than by spiritual affinities. While the present and the early 1960s provide the poles between which the author's perspective constantly oscillates, her memories, connected as they are by constantly evolving human lives, traverse the intervening years as well, and even look back to her life as in impoverished writer in Montreal and Paris.

Each essay is an autonomous work, woven of multiple threads to form a harmonious design. A complex example of Blais's technique is her meditation on the antiwar artists who live in Provincetown in the cold, gray winter of 1963. Far from the bustling crowds of the Cape Cod sum-mer, each artist is isolated in a small house, living only for the colors that lie ready to put on the canvas. The isolation of these artists and their lonely and ultimately impossible fight against war and death mirrors Blais's own situation when a freak accident threatens her with loss of sight in one eye, forcing her to abandon her writing to seek refuge in the play of forms and colors in the natural world around her. And in the background is the presence of Blais's friend Barbara Deming and her hunger strike in a Birmingham prison. Another, very moving chapter weaves together Blais's memories of Jack and Robert, young members of a doomed generation, with the broken and cacophonous music of John Cage heard during a summer in Maine—a sequence of memories of the 1960s that seems to lead inxorably to a vision of the once-boisterous gay community of Provincetown devastated by AIDS in the 1990s.

Although the book's cover terms them "fragments," these essays together evidence a striking coherence of structure and theme. Even more striking is Blais's articulation of a new vision of human life, one that evidences a moving faith in the human capacity to create enduring works of art and meaningful personal relationships. In contrast to portraits of individuals isolated in a repressive and even doomed world, *Parcours d'un écrivain* slowly builds the image of an international community of writers and artists, united by a common devotion to their creative work and a shared opposition to the violence that seems to dominate the world. Blais writes of the bleak time during which she was composing *Une saison dans la vie d'Emmanuel* in a small room in Mary Meigs's Wellfleet home, when the surrounding artistic community becomes for her a spiritual family:

> Dans cette pièce qui me sépare du monde, d'où je sortirai à peine avant la fin de l'hiver, je descendrai en silence dans les vies de Jean-le Maigre et de ses frères, je ne serai pas en meilleure santé mais je me sentirai moins seule dans ma lutte avec tous ces écrivains, ces artistes tout près pour qui l'écriture, la musique, la peinture est le but sacré de leur vie. [In this room that cuts me off from the world, which I rarely leave before the end of the winter, I silently go down into the lives of Jean Le Maigre and his brothers, I am not in any better health but I feel less alone in my struggle with all these writers and artists nearby, for whom writing, music, painting, is the sacred center of their life.] (83).

The existence of this spiritual community of artists and writers is evoked for Blais once again, years later, as she attends the funeral of her friend John Hersey, a jazz funeral like the one they had heard together on the streets of Key West.

Despite the renewed faith in human possibility, death is a dominant element in these essays, as in so many of Blais's books. The presence of death in the volume is much like the author's description of the painting that appears on the cover, a friend's watercolor of a red chair in front of a window with a view of the sea. As Blais interprets the painting, the red chair surrounded by limitless space symbolizes the solitude of the painter, and death is not far away:

La chaise, au milieu d'une étendue d'eau et de ciel, est cette figure de
Diana [Heiskell] elle-même devant le voyage aux portes de l'infini, de
cette mer dont on ne voit pas la fin, aucune extrémité, puisque l'écume de
ses vagues se perd sous le ciel. C'est la mort qui se cache au loin que l'on
ressent déjà toute proche. [The chair, in the midst of a stretch of water
and sky, is the figure of Diana [Heiskell] herself before the voyage to the
gates of the infinite, to this sea whose end is unseen, no limit, since the
spray of its waves is lost under the sky. It is death, hidden in the distance,
that one already senses nearby.] (104)

Each of the brief chapters is centered on a single individual, and most
of them have already passed from Blais's life. Thus each object of Blais's
gaze is portrayed as both present and strangely absent, a double vision
crystallized in the author's encounter with the brother of Blais's friend
Mary McCarthy: in a strange dual image, the eyes and mouth of the living brother re-create the dead sister of whom he speaks. John Kennedy
appears in the text as both a young man on Cape Cod and an assassinated president. Blais writes of Winkie, a woman in Hyannisport paralyzed
by a freak accident in her youth, who evokes her own vivid memory of a
young John F. Kennedy, her friend, who would often come to visit after
her accident, taking hold of her wheelchair and inviting her for a walk
on the beach.

In another essay Blais movingly portrays the despair that overwhelms
the youthful population of Cambridge at the news of Kennedy's death.
In Blais's vision, the deaths of individuals are intensely personal, but
they are not isolated from the larger social context of their time. It is, in
fact, the event of Kennedy's assassination that establishes the tone of the
book, as well as its chronological point of departure, setting the stage for
an "era of massacres" to follow:

Juin 1963: cette année-là un grand président américain sera assassiné,
avec la guerre du Viêt-nam qui approche, chacun de nous assistera à la
télévision, comme dans les journaux, à une ère de massacres traversée parfois de quelques prises de conscience collectives qui changeront le monde.
[June 1963: that year a great American president will be assassinated,
with the approach of the Viet Nam War, each of us will witness on television, as in the newspapers, an era of massacres interrupted from time to
time by a few moments of collective awakening that will change the
world.] (9)

In the background of many of the essays is the racial injustice that
Blais seems to encounter everywhere in the United States, along with

memories of the assassination of civil rights leader Martin Luther King, Jr. During the Vietnam War Blais is moved by her concern for a generation of young men driven to helpless despair, and she is also troubled by her fears for her pacifist friend Barbara Deming as she constantly risks her life and health in her lifelong fight against violence and racial injustice.

Blais's essays are really a series of memoirs, reflections on other lives, and as each essay adds its individual brushstroke to the larger canvas a moving autobiographical work is formed—the most direct and personal statement Blais has made about her experiences. Immersed in a world of artists, Blais seems to suggest a relationship between her essays and the series of sketches she collected in her notebooks of the 1960s:

> Les portraits que je tente de tracer dans mes carnets sont pris sur le vif pendant mes séjours à Cape Cod; ils ne sont que des esquisses peu approfondies, mais je ne veux rien perdre de l'intensité de ces instants que je vis où tant de visages, soudain dans ce nouveau pays, me montrent quelques-uns de leurs traits plus nuancés et plus secrets, à mesure que je m'approche d'eux pour en dessiner les contours. [The portraits I try to set down in my notebooks are taken from life during my stays in Cape Cod; they are only undeveloped sketches, but I don't want to lose any of the intensity of these moments I'm living when so many faces in this new country suddenly reveal to me some of their most nuanced and secret features, as I move closer to them to draw their outlines.] (66)

Chronologically viewed, *Parcours d'un écrivain* takes up Blais's life where the quasi-autobiographical novel *Manuscrits de Pauline Archange* leaves off. At the end of the third volume, Pauline Archange had been left adrift in Quebec City, determined to pursue the project of turning her painful experiences of poverty and oppression into a literary work. At the beginning of *Parcours d'un écrivain* a young Marie-Claire Blais drives from Quebec to Cambridge with her precious typewriter—a typewriter with clear links to the one Pauline Archange had struggled to save from her father's threats of repossession. In *Parcours d'un écrivain* the young writer is freed at last from the demands of menial work by a Guggenheim fellowship and the moral support of Edmund Wilson: she can now devote herself entirely to her writing. In a strange sort of mise-en-abyme, the author of *Parcours d'un écrivain* reveals the way in which her displacement to Cambridge had, in fact, launched the earlier autobiographical project, told through the character of Pauline Archange, as the tragic situation of black Americans in the slums of Cambridge and

Boston had made her more keenly aware of the social oppression of her own Quebec childhood:

> Je tente d'écrire bien maladroitement encore, dans un roman sur les dif-
> férences sociales, ce que je pourrais avoir vu de comparable à la situation
> des Noirs dans la société québécoise, cela qui me perturbe, même à
> l'étranger, le monde des usines où j'ai vu tant de jeunes vies s'étioler,
> s'éteindre pour toujours. (Ce livre qui prendra beaucoup de temps et où il
> sera question du monde des ouvriers deviendra, d'année en année et en
> plusieurs volumes, *Les manuscrits de Pauline Archange.*) [I'm trying to
> write, very clumsily still, in a novel about social differences, what I might
> have seen in Quebec society as comparable to the situation of blacks in
> the United States, which upsets me, even in another country, the world
> of factories in which I have seen so many young lives wither and die.
> (This book, which would take a great deal of time and which would be
> about the world of workers, would become from year to year and in sev-
> eral volumes *The Manuscripts of Pauline Archange.*)] (32)

Blais's experience of liberation in America is not without its own forms of marginalization and pain. Like the deprived Pauline Archange, the still-impoverished Marie-Claire Blais of the 1960s keenly feels her isolation from the privileged Harvard students who lounge on their manicured lawns and the protected world of Edmund Wilson and his family, whose chidren are sent off to Swiss boarding schools rather than condemned to work in factories. Even as she participates in the intellec-tual aristocracy of Cambridge and Wellfleet, the young writer continues to identify with the marginal people who cross her path, the black ado-lescents of the Cambridge ghetto, even those who steal her precious bicycle, and the hapless students who seek refuge from the violence of the surrounding society in ever-more destructive experiments with drugs. Even as she gains access to the sanctuary of Edmund Wilson's pri-vate study, she feels more at ease outside in the living room, in the com-pany of the displaced persons collected by Wilson's émigrée wife, Elena: "Nous sommes tous égaux dans ce salon aux tentures bleues où se calme ma frayeur de ces autres aussi désemparés que moi [We are all at the same level in this living room with its blue drapes where I calm my fear of these others who are as out of place as I am]" (54).

As is suggested by its title, *Parcours d'un écrivain* is, like *Manuscrits de Pauline Archange,* the portrait of an artist, tracing the writer's spiritual itinerary from the moment of her departure from the limited world of her Quebec childhood and her entry into a larger North American intellectual community. Even more than in *Manuscrits,* the trajectory of the writer in *Parcours d'un écrivain* is shaped by her interaction with others. The book is more properly termed a collection of memoirs rather than an autobiography in the traditional form, yet the strands that tie it together form the spiritual itinerary of the author. Like Simone de Beauvoir's *Mémoires d'une jeune fille rangée* and Lillian Hellman's *Pentimento,* the story is told through memories of others, but underlying the successive fragments of memory can be seen the lines of a woman's life and development as a writer.

Although clearly based on the notebooks Blais kept during these years, *Parcours d'un écrivain,* like all true autobiographies, presents a retrospective vision markedly different from that of the notations made by a younger self. The Wellfleet notebooks preserved at the National Library of Canada focus on the progress of Blais's writings and her intellectual apprenticeship in literature and art, set against the troubling background of an America torn by the violence of racial conflict and a destructive Asian war. In contrast, the Blais who writes in 1992 focuses her gaze on people rather than art, on creators rather than their creations. And, although it is centered in a milieu of intellectuals and artists, her world of experience includes those who, through poverty, despair, or devotion to others, have lacked the opportunity for artistic self-expression.

Such a person is the woman to whom the volume is dedicated, Elena Wilson, and the most apparent difference from the earlier notebooks is the shift in focus from an intellectual admiration for Edmund Wilson to an appreciation of the spiritual qualities of his second wife (his former wife, Mary McCarthy, also comes in for praise, although of a different type). The Edmund Wilson of *Parcours d'un écrivain* remains a solicitous godfather, as in earlier texts, but his portraits show greater nuance, perhaps even at times a critical edge. As Blais sits in a Cambridge park on a summer day listening to Wilson discoursing knowledgeably about Virginia Woolf, it is only her own feeling of intellectual inferiority that prevents her from giving vent to the revolt she feels at his appropriation of the woman writer whose marginalized experience, like Blais's, has so little in common with his own self-assurance and masculine privilege. As the young Blais feels more closely identified with an imagined Virginia Woolf than the real man before her, she feels a similar affinity with his wife, Elena, who often invites her to their Wellfleet home. Blais admires the fortitude of the woman who swims in the cold November ocean, and she resonates to the traces of wartime suffering left by a German childhood and, especially, to Elena's Catholic perception of a world of suffering and sainthood. From their first meeting, the young Blais had quarreled with Elena's determination to submit her own life to her husband's, and her last vision of Elena's lonely return to an empty Cape Cod home after her husband's death has a bittersweet quality, lightened in the end by Elena's luminous memory of an earlier time.

Blais's portraits are always tinged with suffering and mortality. Robert, the young black writer she befriends in Cambridge, manages to survive and write, but along the way he abandons a woman companion to a lonely death from cancer and leaves his young wife to kill herself and their baby. The young son of another unhappy couple survives to become a successful artist, but his New York opening is interrupted by the news of his father's suicide. Some of the people Blais meets seem like characters from her early novels, tragically isolated and doomed to an early death. In certain cases, they have come to haunt her imagination, taking form in the pages of her books. This is particularly the case in her novel *David Sterne,* which she reveals as inspired by her Cambridge friends Robert and Jack, the bitterness felt by the young black writer blending with the despair of the young middle-class student confronted by the violence of his world.

Other people, however, are capable of making enduring commitments to personal relationships or to causes involving the whole of humanity, like her friend Barbara Deming, who struggles courageously for peace and racial justice and, in her later years, for feminism. None of the lives who pass before Blais's eyes are free of sadness, and some of her essays focus on the isolation of human life, like the one in which she traces the ironic decomposition of the group of artists gathered around a Cape Cod beachfire. She also offers moving examples of mutual devotion in the face of old age and death: John and Barbara Hersey, Henry and Bessie Poor, and an unnamed but devoted couple of painter and harpsichordist who prepare for her last concert. Elena Wilson's thoughts of her daughter lighten the loneliness of her old age, and the portrait done by Annie Poor of her dying mother preserves the enduring bond between mother and daughter while evoking the image of an entire family united by shared creative concens:

> Annie a peint sa mère comme elle la voyait alors, une mère gracile mais forte, au regard assagi par tant de douleurs, de replis muets: si le corps, la tête ont été rétrécis par le mal, comme s'ils eussent été fondus à la taille

d'un oiseau tombé du nid, une lueur de férocité secourable habite encore l'oeil, le regard est une lampe sans tranquillité qui brille dans les ruines du corps détruit, et cette lampe, c'est l'âme d'Annie, me disais-je en regardant ce tableau dans une galerie de New York, c'est le lien de con-crète durée entre la mère et la fille, entre Bessie et nous qui l'avons con-nue, qui avons lu ses livres. [Annie painted her mother as she saw her then, a mother slender but strong, her gaze made wise by so much grief, so many mute withdrawals: if the body, the head have been shrunken by illness, as if they had been melted down to the size of a bird fallen from the nest, a gleam of amiable ferocity still lurks in the eye, her gaze is a restless lamp that burns in the ruins of the devastated body, and that lamp is Annie's soul, I said to myself in front of the painting in a New York art gallery, it is the concrete bond of continuity between the moth-er and the daughter, between Bessie and those of us who knew her, who read her books.] (205–6)

In her decision to ground her essays, and her life, in a community of writers and artists, Blais offers a new understanding of the meaning of art. No longer simply the means to personal salvation it had been for Pauline Archange, writing becomes for Blais her only possible response to the violence and despair that seem to surround her:

Comment écrire autre chose que l'injustice ressentie quand on vit dans une atmosphère si chargée de rumeurs de guerre, de brutalité, de racisme aussi outrageusement exprimé? J'essaie pourtant d'écrire tous les jours, et ce geste me paraît le seul geste décent et utile que je puisse accomplir pendant ces mois d'appréhension où les étudiants sur tous les campus américains manifestent leurs craintes de la guerre au Viêt-nam. [How can you write about anything other than the injustice you feel when you live in an atmosphere filled with rumblings of war, of brutality, of racism, so outrageously expressed? But I try to write every day, and that seems to me the only decent, useful act I can make during these months of appre-hension when the students on all the campuses in America are demon-strating their fears about the war in Vietnam.] (66)

Blais's descriptions of the multiple portraits of self and others painted by her friend Mary Meigs provides a sort of commentary on her essays. The series of self-portraits Meigs describes in their first conversation in the Fogg Art Museum in Cambridge is certainly a model for her own quest for self-understanding. Her gaze turned to others rather than focused on herself, Blais's method in this volume is perhaps more like the multiple portraits of family members that Meigs later undertakes, using the various visions of a single person as the basis for a final composite portrait that encompasses them all. As in Meigs's work, the same figures recur in Blais's essays at different moments of their lives—Jack and Robert, Elena and Edmund Wilson—providing the unifying themes of an only apparently fragmented work. The layering of different moments of time is an explicit part of the structure of this work, built up of different moments in time, and Blais's description of Meigs's final portrait of her father could serve as an emblem of Blais's project:

> Digne et résigné, il attend; mais par des touches méticuleuses, l'enfance, la jeunesse de l'homme atteint de tuberculose encore jeune, dans cette sensualité des couleurs qui baigne le tableau, autour de la tête pensive du père, des époques glorieuses, des instants peut-être semblent courir autour de lui dans un flot d'images arrêtées, le voici petit garçon aux côtés de ses frères, tout endimanché pour une photographie qui semble venir d'un autre siècle ou habillé pour une promenade à cheval, plus tard, avec sa femme et ses enfants; sa seule certitude, pendant que ses yeux bleus nous fixent, c'est que ce monde tel qu'il l'a connu, ce monde vivant, jamais ne reviendra plus. [Dignified and resigned, he waits; but through meticulous details, the childhood and youth of the man afflicted with tuberculosis while still young, in that sensuality of colors that bathes the painting, around the father's pensive head, glorious eras, moments perhaps seem to surround him in a flow of frozen images, here he is as a little boy with his brothers, dressed up for a photo that seems to come from another century or dressed for an outing on horseback, later, with his wife and children; his only certainty, as his blue eyes transfix us, is that the world as he knew it, that living world will never return.] (91)

The itinerary Blais inscribes is an apprenticeship in art and in life, and the teachers she describes are primarily women. While she thinks of Rimbaud and Keats as she creates Jean Le Maigre, she seeks sustenance in reading the Spanish-language writers Rosalia Castro and Gabriela Mistral, introduced to her by Meigs, and in the work of Mary McCarthy:

> Je me demande par quel miracle ces oeuvres ont été écrites par des femmes, sous le déguisement poétique ou romanesque, j'admire l'incroyable bravoure de ces auteurs lorsqu'elles parlent d'elles-mêmes avec une telle franchise. [I wonder by what miracle those works have been written by women, behind their poetic or romanesque form, I admire the incredible bravery of those daring authors when they speak of themselves so openly.] (82)

Blais is also moved by McCarthy's political commitment when, along with Robert Lowell, she goes to Vietnam to protest the bombing of Hanoi. It is through McCarthy that she will come to know the feminist writer Monique Wittig, whose *L'Opoponax,* the story of a girl's experience, is not unlike her own *Manuscrits de Pauline Archange.*

It is Blais's growing identification with women and especially the North American "feminist revolution" of the late 1960s that constitutes a source of tension in her relationship with Edmund Wilson: as she comments, "Edmund et moi n'entendons pas la même musique [Edmund and I don't hear the same music]" (52). Blais actively questions Wilson's inability to understand that his friends and neighbors, Meigs and Deming, have chosen a life without husband and children. For Blais, her friends, their lives as independent women living without a man, are a source of inspiration, "des voix singulières que je peux entendre et qui refusent de se soumettre [independent voices I can understand and who refuse to give in]" (61). Meigs and Deming also represent for her a life of creativity and commitment. Blais comments on the ability of Deming to remain at her writing all day, with barely a pause, and she admires the rigorous daily schedule established by Meigs, who divides her time between painting, perfecting her command of Spanish, and playing the flute.

Many of the creative artists of whom Blais writes are women—the painter whose studio she visits in Cambridge, the aging harpsichordist slowly losing her battle with blindness, the aging American poet Hortense Flexner, taken out of her nursing home to have tea once again with her translator, the French writer Marguerite Yourcenar. Blais writes of her artist friend Francese, who, inspired by a pioneering woman orchestra conductor, takes up the practice of sculpture at the age of 60. In Francese's battle with the resistant matter of stone and metal, Blais embodies the struggle of women to enter a field of achievement formerly reserved for men. The courage of the women Blais describes is not limited to artists and writers. The strong figure of Elena Wilson, with her unusual beauty, recurs throughout the essays, and Blais admires the tenacity of her paralyzed friend Winkie, along with the devotion of her companion, Gigi.

For the Blais of the 1960s, tormented by the ambient violence and the constant assassinations of national figures, their widows provide an emblem of the nation's grief and a source of hope for a different world:

> Pendant ces jours de deuil et de tueries, ces figures de femmes, veuve d'un président, d'un pasteur, sous leurs voiles noirs, viendront tourmenter

notre mémoire; dans ces femmes, chacun reconnaîtra un peu de son cha-
grin. Nous porterons avec elles le fardeau de la séparation, elles incar-
neront aussi pour la jeunesse la maternité qui pleure, celle qui met au
monde la vie, et non la mort, la violence qu'a engendrées l'homme.
[During these days of mourning and killing, these faces of women, widow
of a president, a pastor, under their black veils, will return to torment our
memory; in these women, each of us will recognize a little of our grief.
We will bear with them the burden of separation, they will also incarnate, in the eyes of youth, a grieving motherhood which gives birth to life
and not to the death and violence engendered by man.] (59)

Some of the women Blais describes have failed in their attempts, like the
mad sister of Tennessee Williams, whose memory survives in Key West.
But the collection ends with the image of a young woman who aspires to
make her mark in the world of sailing by captaining her own racing
crew. It is her optimistic words that conclude the book: "Les voiles sont
mises . . . c'est notre tour maintenant [The sails are set . . . it's our turn
now]" (217).

Notes and References

Chapter One

1. Robertson Davies, "A Season in the Life of Emmanuel," *New York Times Book Review*, 21 August 1966, 28.
2. Edmund Wilson, *O Canada: An American's Notes on Canadian Culture* (New York: Noonday Press/Farrar, Straus & Giroux, 1964), 148; hereafter cited in text.
3. Much documentation about Blais's family is provided by Thérèse Fabi in *Le Monde perturbé des jeunes dans l'oeuvre de Marie-Claire Blais* (Montreal: Editions Agence d'Arc, 1973).
4. For Mary Meigs's account of Blais, see *The Medusa Head* (Vancouver: Talonbooks, 1983) and *Lily Briscoe: A Self-Portrait* (Vancouver: Talonbooks, 1981).
5. Much information about Blais's years in Wellfleet and Cambridge appears in her memoirs, *Parcours d'un écrivain: Notes américaines* (Montreal: VLB Editeur, 1993); hereafter cited in text with my translation.
6. "L'Amie révolutionnaire," in *L'Exilé* (Montreal: Bibliothèque Québécoise, 1992), 46–56; hereafter cited in text with my translation.
7. Blais's notebooks are located in the Canadian National Library in Ottawa.
8. Margaret Atwood, "Marie-Claire Blais Is Not for Burning," *Maclean's*, September 1975, 28.

Chapter Two

1. See, for example, the interview with Blais in *La Patrie,* 10 April 1960, 7.
2. For example, Joseph d'Anjou, *Relations,* no. 229 (January 1960): 22.
3. See, for example, Joan Coldwell, "Mad Shadows as Psychological Fiction," *Journal of Canadian Fiction* 2, no. 4 (1973): 65–67.
4. Gilles Marcotte, "Marie-Claire Blais, romancière et poète," *Le Devoir,* 31 October 1959; my translation.
5. Guy Fournier, "Comment l'auteur voit son roman, *La Belle Bête,*" *Perspectives*, 2 January 1960.
6. Goldmann's analysis was published as "Note sur deux romans de Marie-Claire Blais," in *Structures mentales et création culturelle* (Paris: Editions Anthropos, 1970), 353–64; hereafter cited in text with my translation. See also

the interview with Goldmann by Alain Pontaut, "La Littérature n'est-elle qu'un fait social?" *La Presse,* 11 February 1967.

7.   For a further development of this theme, see my article "Redefining the Maternal: Women's Relationships in the Fiction of Marie-Claire Blais" in *Traditionalism, Nationalism, and Feminism: Women Writers of Quebec,* ed. Paula Gilbert Lewis (Westport, Conn.: Greenwood Press, 1985), 125–39.

8.   Louis Hémon, *Maria Chapdelaine* (Montreal: Bibliothèque Canadienne-Française, 1975), 213; my translation.

9.   Margaret Atwood, "Québec: Burning Mansions," in *Survival: A Thematic Guide to Canadian Literature* (Toronto: Anansi, 1972), 213–31.

10.   For a study of mirroring, see Douglas H. Parker, "The Shattered Glass: Mirror and Illusion in *Mad Shadows,*" *Journal of Canadian Fiction* 2, no. 4 (1973): 68–70.

11.   Beatrice Slama suggests a similar interpretation in her article "*La Belle Bête,* ou la double scène," *Voix et Images* 8 (Winter 1983): 213–28.

12.   *La Belle Bête* (1959; Montreal: Pierre Tisseyre, 1977), 35; *Mad Shadows,* trans. Merloyd Lawrence (Toronto: McClelland & Stewart, 1971), 33; both hereafter cited in text.

13.   Blais's rewriting of fairy tales is discussed by several critics, most notably Jennifer Waelti-Walters in her chapter "'Cinderella' and *Mad Shadows* (Blais)," in *Fairy Tales and the Female Imagination* (Montreal: Eden Press, 1982), 45–57. See also Barbara Godard, "Blais' *La Belle Bête:* Infernal Fairy Tale," in *Violence in the Canadian Novel,* ed. Virginia Harger Grinling and Terry Goldie (St. John's: St. John's Memorial University, 1981), 159–75, and Slama, "*La Belle Bête,* ou la double scène."

Chapter Three

1.   *Une Saison dans la vie d'Emmanuel* (1965; Montreal: Editions Quinze, 1978), 7; *A Season in the Life of Emmanuel,* trans. Derek Coltman, introduction by Edmund Wilson (1966; New York: Farrar, Straus & Giroux, 1980), 3–4; both hereafter cited in text.

2.   Several critics have located a number of precise references to Rimbaud's work, such as Jean Le Maigre's preoccupation with lice, a possible reference to Rimbaud's poem "Les Chercheuses de poux." See Elaine D. Cancalon "*Une saison dans la vie d'Emmanuel:* Le Discours du conte," *Voix et Images* 43 (Fall 1989): 105.

3.   *Le Figaro,* 4 April 1966, 13; reprinted in *Le Devoir,* 12 April 1966, 10.

4.   Gilles Marcotte, *Le Roman à l'imparfait* (Montreal: La Presse, 1976), 126.

5.   Henri Mitterand, "Coup de pistolet dans un concert: *Une saison dans la vie d'Emmanuel,*" *Voix et Images* 2 (April 1977): 407–17.

6.   "Remerciements simples et confus à ses jurés," *L'Action,* 30 November 1966; my translation.

7. "Testament de Jean-le Maigre à ses frères," *Liberté* 81 (1972): 74–83.

Chapter Four

1. *Tête Blanche* (1960; Montreal: Editions de l'Actuelle, 1977), 130; *Tête Blanche,* trans. Charles Fullman (Toronto: McClelland & Stewart, New Canadian Library No. 104, 1983), 86; both hereafter cited in text.
2. Scott Symons, "Marie-Claire Blais: L'Autopse du Québec aux yeux d'un torontois," *La Presse,* March 1961.
3. André Belleau, "Epilogue à une querelle," *Liberté* 3, no. 2 (1961): 455.
4. *David Sterne* (Montreal: Stanké, Collection Québec 10/10, 1981), 220; hereafter cited in text with my translation.
5. Interview in *Le Devoir,* 21 July 1984, 21; my translation.
6. *Pierre, ou la guerre du printemps 1981* (1984; Montreal: Boréal, 1991), 12–13; hereafter cited in text with my translation.
7. Nancy Chodorow, *The Reproduction of Mothering* (Berkeley and Los Angeles: University of California Press, 1978).

Chapter Five

1. Gabrielle Frémont, "*Le Jour est noir,* roman de Marie-Claire Blais," *Dictionnaire des oeuvres littéraires du Québec* (Montreal: Fides, 1980–87), 4: 480.
2. *Le Jour est noir suivi de L'Insoumise* (1966; Montreal: Stanké, Collection Québec 10/10, 1979), 49; *The Day Is Dark,* trans. Derek Coltman (New York: Farrar, Straus & Giroux, 1966), 44; both hereafter cited in text.
3. Gilles Marcotte, "Le Troisième Roman de Marie-Claire Blais," *La Presse,* 10 February 1962, 8.
4. "'Suis à la mer . . . écris beaucoup . . . très heureuse'" (interview with Gérald Godin), *Maclean's,* May 1966, 71.
5. *Le Jour est noir suivi de L'Insoumise* (1966; Montreal: Stanké, Collection Québec 10/10, 1979), 191–92; *The Fugitive,* trans. David Lobdell (Ottawa: Oberon Press, 1978), 58; both hereafter cited in text.
6. *Le Loup* (1972; Montreal: Boréal, 1990), 9; *The Wolf,* trans. Sheila Fischman (Toronto: McClelland & Stewart, 1974), 7; both hereafter cited in text.
7. Victor-Laurent Tremblay, "L'Art de la fugue dans *Le Loup* de Marie-Claire Blais," *French Review* 59, no. 6 (May 1986): 911–20. Tremblay goes on to give a detailed analysis of the way in which the fugal structure is worked out in each of the four sections of Blais's text.
8. In *The Medusa Head* Blais's longtime companion, Mary Meigs, says Blais, much like her protagonist, regarded "all her great loves" as "a work of salvation" (11).

9. Adrienne Rich, *Of Woman Born: Motherhood as Experience and Institution* (New York: Bantam, 1981), 257.

Chapter Six

1. Quoted in *Le Devoir,* 9 March 1968.
2. Alonzo Leblanc, "L'Exécution, drame de Marie-Claire Blais," *Dictionnaire des oeuvre s littéraires du Québec,* 330; hereafter cited in text.
3. Jennifer Waelti-Walters, "Guilt: The Prison of This World," *Canadian Literature* 88 (Spring 1981): 50.
4. *Le Devoir,* 9 March 1968.
5. *L'Exécution* (Montreal: Editions du Jour, 1968), 115; *The Execution,* trans. David Lobdell (Vancouver: Talonbooks, 1976), 100; both hereafter cited in text.
6. Laurent Mailhot, "L'Exécution de Marie-Claire Blais," in *Livres et auteurs québécois* (Quebec: Presses de l'Université Laval, 1969), 72.
7. *Le Devoir,* 23 April 1988, C-1.
8. "L'Envahisseur," "Le Disparu," "Deux Destins," "Fièvre," and "Un Couple" were published in *Fièvre et autres textes dramatiques: Théâtre radiophonique* (Montreal: Editions du Jour, 1974); hereafter cited in text with my translation.
9. In its best-known form, this legend appears as the story of Rose Latulippe in *L'Influence d'un livre* (1837) by Philippe Aubert de Gaspé fils, considered the first French-Canadian novel.
10. In *Sommeil d'hiver* (Montreal: Editions de la Pleine Lune, 1984), 90; hereafter cited in text with my translation.
11. Paula Gilbert Lewis, "Les Textes dramatiques radiophoniques de Marie-Claire Blais," *Québec Studies* 10 (1990): 37–43.

Chapter Seven

1. *Manuscrits de Pauline Archange* (1968; Montreal: Stanké, Collection Québec 10/10, 1981), 208; *The Manuscripts of Pauline Archange,* trans. Derek Coltman (Toronto: McClelland & Stewart, New Canadian Library, 1982), 106; both hereafter cited in text.
2. James Kraft makes a similar comparison in "Fiction as Autobiography in Québec: Notes on Pierre Vallières and Marie-Claire Blais," *Novel* 6, no. 1 (Fall 1972): 73–78.
3. This aspect of Blais's work is discussed in my article "Structures of Liberation: Female Experience and Autobiographical Form in Quebec," *Yale French Studies* 65 (1983): 124–36, reprinted in *Life/Lines,* ed. Celeste Schenck and Bella Brodzki (Ithaca, N.Y.: Cornell University Press, 1989).
4. This statement was quoted by Christiane Makward in her article "Quebec Women Writers," *Women and Literature* 7 (Winter 1979): 3. Brossard's remarks were reprinted in *Liberté* 18 (July–October 1976): 13.

5. Yvan G. Lepage, "*Vivre! Vivre!* de Marie-Claire Blais," in *Livres et auteurs québécois,* 174.

6. Roger Duhamel, "*Manuscrits de Pauline Archange* de Marie-Claire Blais," in *Livres et auteurs québécois,* 41.

7. Estelle C. Jelinek, ed., *Women's Autobiography: Essays in Criticism* (Bloomington: Indiana University Press, 1980), 17, 19.

8. Mary G. Mason, "The Other Voice: Autobiographies of Women Writers," in *Women's Autobiography,* 10.

9. Domna C. Stanton, ed., *The Female Autograph* (Chicago: University of Chicago Press, 1984), 15.

10. See Karen Gould, "The Censored Word and the Body Politic: Reconsidering the Fiction of Marie-Claire Blais," *Journal of Popular Culture* 15, no. 3 (Winter 1981): 14–27.

11. *Vivre! Vivre!* (1969; Montreal: Stanké, Collection Québec 10/10, 1981), 13–14; *The Manuscripts of Pauline Archange,* trans. Derek Coltman (Toronto: McClelland & Stewart, New Canadian Library, 1982), 110; both hereafter cited in text.

12. *Les Apparences* (1970; Montreal: Stanké, Collection Québec 10/10, 1981), 148; *Dürer's Angel,* trans. David Lobdell (Vancouver: Talon books, 1976), 77.

Chapter Eight

1. Margaret Atwood, Introduction to *St. Lawrence Blues,* trans. Ralph Manheim (Toronto: McClelland & Stewart, 1985), x; hereafter cited in text.

2. Quoted in Lise Gauvin, *Parti pris littéraire* (Montreal: Presses de l'Université de Montréal, 1975), 63. For an excellent discussion of the linguistic debate over *joual,* see Chapter 3, pp. 55–74.

3. See, in particular, the reviews of Réginald Martel, "Nous sommes tous des trous-de-cul," *La Presse,* 19 May 1973, D3, and Ivanhoé Beaulieu, *Le Devoir,* 2 June 1973, 15.

4. *Un Joualonais sa Joualonie* (Montreal: Stanké, Collection Québec 10/10, 1979), 143; hereafter cited in text.

5. This sentence was pointed out by Barbara Godard in her article "La Grande Querelle," *Journal of Canadian Fiction* 3, no. 3 (1974): 106–8.

6. The identification of *Un Joualonais* as picaresque is made by, among others, Howard Roiter, "Down Weirdo Road with a Blais Picarole," *Globe and Mail,* 18 August 1973, 28, and Gary Werder, "Realism Picaresque Pseudo-Confession," *Canadian Literature* (Winter 1976): 109–12.

7. *Une liaison parisienne* (Montreal: Stanké, Collection Québec 10/10, 1982), 63; *A Literary Affair,* trans. Sheila Fischman (Toronto: McClelland & Stewart, 1979), 60; both hereafter cited in text.

8. Gabrielle Poulin, "Une saison dans la vie des Français," *Lettres Québécoises,* no. 2 (May 1976): 3–5.

9. See also Meigs's *Lily Briscoe: A Self-Portrait.*

Chapter Nine

1.   Quoted by Monique Roy, "Marie-Claire Blais: 'Chaque livre est un engagement,'" *Le Devoir,* 4 March 1978, 33; hereafter cited in text with my translation.

2.   *La Nef des sorcières* (Ottawa: Quinze, 1976), 7; hereafter cited in text with my translation.

3.   *Les Nuits de l'Underground* (Ottawa: Stanké, 1978), 10; *Nights in the Underground,* trans. Ray Ellenwood (Toronto: General Publishing Co./Newpress Canadian Classics, 1982), 1; both hereafter cited in text.

4.   Coral Ann Howells, *Private and Fictional Worlds: Canadian Women Novelists of the 1970s and 1980s* (London and New York: Methuen, 1987), 160; hereafter cited in text.

5.   Gilles Marcotte, "Une saison dans la vie de Geneviève Aurès," *Le Devoir,* 25 March 1978, 35.

6.   Although Blais does not make this reference explicit, *L'Etoile rose* is the title of a novel published in 1978 by Dominique Fernandez which recounts the experiences of a French homosexual of Blais's generation and contrasts them with the more liberated life of his younger lover.

7.   *L'Ange de la solitude* (Montreal: VLB Editeur, 1989), 111; hereafter cited in text with my translation.

8.   This exchange took place in a public forum at the Congrès International d'Etudes Francophones in New Orleans, April 1988.

Chapter Ten

1.   *Le Sourd dans la ville* (Montreal: Stanké, 1979), 18; *Deaf to the City,* trans. Carol Dunlop (Woodstock, N.Y.: Overlook Press, 1987), 12; both hereafter cited in text.

2.   Carol Gilligan, *In a Different Voice* (Cambridge, Mass.: Harvard University Press, 1982), 57.

Chapter Eleven

1.   *Visions d'Anna, ou le vertige* (1982; Montreal: Boréal Compact 22, 1990), 206; *Anna's World,* trans. Sheila Fischman (Toronto: Lester & Orpen Dennys, 1985), 176; both hereafter cited in text.

2.   Julia Kristeva, *About Chinese Women,* trans. Anita Barrows (New York, London: Marion Boyars, 1986), 34.

3.   Paula Gilbert Lewis comments on this scene in her article, "From Shattered Reflections to Female Bonding: Mirroring in Marie-Claire Blais's *Visions d'Anna,*" *Québec Studies* 2 (1984): 94–104.

4.   Marie Couillard, "*Visions d'Anna,* ou l'écriture du vertige de Marie-Claire Blais," *Québec Studies* 17 (1993–94): 117–24.

Selected Bibliography

PRIMARY WORKS

Books

L'Ange de la solitude. Montreal: VLB Editeur, 1989.

La Belle Bête. 1959. Montreal: Pierre Tisseyre, 1977. Translated as *Mad Shadows* by Merloyd Lawrence. Toronto: McClelland & Stewart, 1971.

David Sterne. 1967. Montreal: Stanké, Collection Québec 10/10, 1981.

L'Exécution. Montreal: Editions du Jour, 1968. Translated as *The Execution* by David Lobdell. Vancouver: Talonbooks, 1976.

L'Exilé: nouvelles suivi de Les Voyageurs sacrés. Montreal: Boréal, 1992. *Les Voyageurs sacrés* (1966) translated as *The Three Travellers* by Derek Coltman. Toronto: Penguin, 1966, 1985.

Fièvre et autres textes dramatiques: Théâtre radiophonique. Montreal: Editions du Jour, 1974.

L'Ile. Montreal: VLB, 1988.

Le Jour est noir suivi de L'Insoumise. 1961 and 1966. Montreal: Stanké, Collection Québec 10/10, 1979. *Le Jour est noir* translated as *The Day Is Dark* by Derek Coltman. Toronto: Penguin, 1985. *L'Insoumise* translated as *The Fugitive* by David Lobdell. Ottawa: Oberon Press, 1978.

Le Loup. 1972. Montreal: Boréal, 1990. Translated as *The Wolf* by Sheila Fischman. Toronto: McClelland & Stewart, 1974.

Manuscrits de Pauline Archange. 1968. Montreal: Stanké, Collection Québec 10/10, 1981. *Vivre! Vivre!* 1969. Montreal: Stanké, Collection Québec 10/10, 1981. *Les Apparences.* 1970. Montreal: Stanké, Collection Québec 10/10, 1981. The first two volumes translated as *The Manuscripts of Pauline Archange* by Derek Coltman. Toronto: McClelland & Stewart, New Canadian Library, 1982. The third volume translated as *Dürer's Angel* by David Lobdell. Vancouver: Talonbooks, 1976.

Les Nuits de l'Underground. Ottawa: Stanké, 1978. Translated as *Nights in the Underground* by Ray Ellenwood. Toronto: General Publishing Co./Newpress Canadian Classics, 1982.

L'Océan suivi de Murmures. Montreal: Les Editions Quinze, 1977.

Parcours d'un écrivain: Notes américaines. Montreal: VLB Editeur, 1993.

Pays voilés—existences. Montreal: Stanké, Collection Quebec 10/10, 1983. Translated as *Veiled countries/lives* by Michael Harris. Toronto: Véhicule, 1984, 1988.

Pierre, ou la guerre du printemps 1981. 1984. Montreal; Boréal, 1991.

Sommeil d'hiver. Montreal: Editions de la Pleine Lune, 1984.

Le Sourd dans la ville. Montreal: Stanké, 1979. Translated as *Deaf to the City* by Carol Dunlop. Woodstock, N.Y.: Overlook Press, 1987.

Tête Blanche. 1960. Montreal: Editions de l'Actuelle, 1977. Translated as *Tête Blanche* by Charles Fullman. Toronto: McClelland & Stewart, New Canadian Library, 1983.

Une liaison parisienne. 1976. Montreal: Stanké, Collection Québec 10/10, 1982. Translated as *A Literary Affair* by Sheila Fischman. Toronto: McClelland & Stewart, 1979.

Une saison dans la vie d'Emmanuel. 1965. Montreal: Editions Quinze, 1978. Translated as *A Season in the Life of Emmanuel* by Derek Coltman, introduction by Edmund Wilson. New York: Farrar, Straus & Giroux, 1966, 1980.

Un Joualonais sa Joualonie. 1973. Montreal: Stanké, Collection Québec 10/10, 1979. Translated as *St. Lawrence Blues* by Ralph Manheim. Toronto: McClelland & Stewart, 1985.

Visions d'Anna, ou le vertige. 1982. Montreal: Boréal, 1990. Translated as *Anna's World* by Sheila Fischman. Toronto: Lester & Orpen Dennys, 1985.

Other Works

"Marcelle." In *La Nef des sorcières,* edited by Nicole Brossard and France Théoret. Ottawa: Quinze, 1976.

"Testament de Jean-le Maigre à ses frères." *Liberté* 81 (1972): 74–83.

SECONDARY WORKS

Bibliographies

Boivin, Aurélien; Lucie Robert; and Ruth Major-Lapierre. "Bibliographie de Marie-Claire Blais." *Voix et Images* 8 (Winter 1983): 248–95.

Ricouart, Janine. "Bibliographie sur Marie-Claire Blais." *Québec Studies* 10 (1990): 51–60.

Books

Fabi, Thérèse. *Le Monde perturbé des jeunes dans l'oeuvre de Marie-Claire Blais.* Montreal: Editions Agence d'Arc, 1973. Still unsurpassed for its insight into Blais's biography. Also provides brief analyses of Blais's novels through *Manuscrits de Pauline Archange.* Includes a useful bibliography.

Laurent, Françoise. *L'Oeuvre romanesque de Marie-Claire Blais.* Montreal: Fides, 1986. A systematic study of Blais's novels, stressing their grounding in universal themes as well as the poetic nature of Blais's writing.

Meigs, Mary. *Lily Briscoe: A Self-Portrait.* Vancouver: Talonbooks, 1981. Dedicated to Barbara Deming and Marie-Claire Blais, this autobiographical work traces the author's life with Blais on Cape Cod.

————. *The Medusa Head.* Vancouver: Talonbooks, 1983. A second volume of Meigs's autobiography, it recounts the real-life love triangle treated by Blais in *Une liaison parisienne.*

Nadeau, Vincent. *Marie-Claire Blais: Le Noir et le tendre. Etude d'Une saison dans la vie d'Emmanuel, suivi d'une bibliographie critique.* Montreal: Les Presses de l'Université de Montréal, 1974. As suggested by its title, this study sees *Une saison dans la vie d'Emmanuel* as a mixture of black pessimism and human tenderness.

Northey, Margot. *The Haunted Wilderness,* 70–78. Toronto: University of Toronto Press, 1976. Reads *La Belle Bête* as a variant of the gothic, with its atmosphere of degeneration and menacing evil.

Paradis, Suzanne. *Femme fictive, femme réelle: Le Personnage féminin dans le roman féminin canadien français (1884–1966).* Quebec: Editions Garneau, 1966. This pioneering book on Quebec women writers focuses on their women characters. Discusses *La Belle Bête, Tête Blanche, Le Jour est noir, Une saison dans la vie d'Emmanuel,* and *L'Insoumise.*

Stratford, Philip. *Canadian Writers and Their Works: Marie-Claire Blais.* Toronto: Forum House Publishing Co., 1971. Offers an insightful study of all Blais's work through *Manuscrits de Pauline Archange.*

Articles and Parts of Books

Ahmed, Maroussia. "La Technique de l'inversion dans les romans de Marie-Claire Blais." *Canadian Modern Language Review* 31, no. 5 (May 1975): 380–86. Shows how Blais's protagonists effect a reversal of the traditional Quebec value system.

Brûlé, Michel. "Introduction à l'univers de Marie-Claire Blais." *Revue de l'Institut de Sociologie, Bruxelles,* no. 3 (1969): 503–13. In the wake of Lucien Goldmann, sees Blais's first five novels as related to the era of contestation in Quebec's Quiet Revolution.

Cagnon, Maurice. "Marie-Claire Blais." In *The French Novel of Quebec,* 106–12. Boston: Twayne Publishers, 1986. Comments on Blais's major novels as illustrating her solicitude and pity for marginal, tormented, or alienated characters.

Callaghan, Barry. "An Interview with Marie-Claire Blais." *Tamarack Review* 37 (Fall 1965): 29–34. Interview at Blais's home on Cape Cod just before the publication of *Une saison dans la vie d'Emmanuel.*

Cancalon, Elaine D. "*Une saison dans la vie d'Emmanuel:* Le Discours du conte." *Voix et Images* 43 (Fall 1989): 102–10. Explores *Une saison dans la vie d'Emmanuel* as a mixture of narrative genres.

Cliche, Elène. "Un rituel de l'avidité." *Voix et Images* 8 (Winter 1983): 229–47. A study of new directions in Blais's writing, especially her use of intertextuality in *Les Nuits de l'Underground, Le Sourd dans la ville,* and *Visions d'Anna.*

Coldwell, Joan. "*Mad Shadows* as Psychological Fiction." *Journal of Canadian Fiction* 2, no. 4 (1973): 65–67. Reads *La Belle Bête* as a projection onto the external world of acts generally confined to private fantasy, stressing references to myth and fairy tale.

Couillard, Marie. "Ecrire et vivre au Québec des femmes: Impression et expression d'une culture." *North Dakota Quarterly* 52, no. 3 (Summer 1984): 87–99. Describes process of mythification of masculine and feminine characters in Quebec literature and their demystification at the hands of women novelists of the 1960s and 1970s, especially Blais and Anne Hébert.

———. "Les Carnets de Marie-Claire Blais: Du privé au public." *Québec Studies* 10 (1990): 1–8. An overview of the contents of Blais's notebooks from the years 1962 to 1974, in the archives of the Canadian National Library.

———. "*Visions d'Anna,* ou l'écriture du vertige de Marie-Claire Blais." *Québec Studies* 17 (1993–94): 117–24. Analysis of patterns of meaning in *Visions d'Anna.*

Davis, Marilyn I. "*La Belle Bête:* Pilgrim unto Life." *Tamarack Review* 16 (Summer 1960): 51–59. Stresses allegorical aspects of *La Belle Bête* as representation of the soul of Quebec.

Dawson, Anthony B. "Coming of Age in Canada." *Mosaic* 11, no. 3 (Spring 1978): 47–62. Argues for a distinctly Canadian vision of coming of age, as a movement from certainty to uncertainty, as seen in W. O. Mitchell, Margaret Laurence, Alice Munro, and Blais.

Falardeau, Jean-Charles, "The Evolution of the Hero in the Quebec Novel." *Contemporary Quebec Criticism,* edited by Larry Shouldice, 95–116. Toronto: University of Toronto Press, 1979. Places Blais's heroes in the context of the evolution of Quebec literature.

Godard, Barbara. "Blais' *La Belle Bête:* Infernal Fairy Tale." In *Violence in the Canadian Novel since 1960/Violence dans le roman canadien depuis 1960,* edited by Virginia Harger Grinling and Terry Goldie, 159–75. St. John's: St. John's Memorial University, 1981. A study of Blais's inversion of the basic elements of the fairy tale in *La Belle Bête,* with an extension of the analysis to other novels.

———. "La Grande Querelle." *Journal of Canadian Fiction* 3, no. 3 (1974): 106–8. Stresses the humor and parodic elements in *Un Joualonais sa Joualonie.*

Goldmann, Lucien. "Note sur deux romans de Marie-Claire Blais." In *Structures Mentales et création culturelle,* 353–64. Paris: Editions Anthropos, 1970. A sociological reading of *La Belle Bête* and *Une saison dans la vie d'Emmanuel,* which sees them as expressions of the revolt of young Quebec intellectuals against a repressive, traditional society.

Gordon, Jan. "An 'Incandescence of Suffering': The Fiction of Marie-Claire Blais." *Modern Fiction Studies* 22, no. 3 (Fall 1976): 468–79. Analyzes various factors that contribute to the dark world of Blais's fiction.

Gould, Karen. "The Censored Word and the Body Politic: Reconsidering the Fiction of Marie-Claire Blais." *Journal of Popular Culture,* 15, no. 3 (Winter 1981): 14–27. Suggests relationship between the censorship of women's bodies and the silencing of their language in *Manuscrits de Pauline Archange* and *Les Nuits de l'Underground.*

Green, Mary Jean. "Redefining the Maternal: Women's Relationships in the Fiction of Marie-Claire Blais." In *Traditionalism, Nationalism, and Feminism: Women Writers of Quebec,* edited by Paula Gilbert Lewis, 125–39. Westport, Conn.: Greenwood Press, 1985. A study of the evolution in Blais's portrayal of relationships among women, from the hostile mother-daughter relationships of her early work to a perspective that sees mutual caring among women as a source of hope in the world.

———. "Structures of Liberation: Female Experience and Autobiographical Form in Quebec." *Yale French Studies* 65 (1983): 124–36. Reprinted in *Life/Lines,* edited by Celeste Schenck and Bella Brodzki. Ithaca, N.Y.: Cornell University Press, 1989. Looks at Blais's *Manuscrits de Pauline Archange* and Claire Martin's *Dans un gant de fer* in the context of women's autobiography.

Green, Mary Jean; Paula Gilbert Lewis; and Karen Gould. "Inscriptions of the Feminine: A Century of Women Writing in Quebec." *American Review of Canadian Studies* 15, no. 4 (1985): 363–87. Traces the history of women's writing in Quebec through the contributions of major figures; Paula Gilbert Lewis discusses representations of the feminine in silence and language in *Visions d'Anna.*

Herden, Martin. "Le Monologue intérieur dans *The Sound and the Fury* de William Faulkner et *Le Sourd dans la ville* de Marie-Claire Blais." *Voix et Images* 42 (Spring 1989): 483–96. Finds striking parallels between Blais's text and Quentin's interior monologue in *The Sound and the Fury,* despite differences in focus.

Howells, Coral Ann. "Marie-Claire Blais, *Les Nuits de l'Underground;* Anne Hébert, *Héloïse.*" In *Private and Fictional Worlds: Canadian Women Novelists of the 1970s and 1980s,* 157–72. London and New York: Methuen, 1987. In the context of a larger study of Canadian women's writing, sees Blais's portrayal of lesbians who are also Québécoises as an expression of women's struggle for identity.

Iqbal, Françoise. "Sur-vivre et sous-vivre: La Sexualité dans *Une saison dans la vie d'Emmanuel.*" *Incidences,* n.s. 4, nos. 2–3 (May–December 1980): 85–99. Sees sexual repression as related to failure of children's development in *Une saison dans la vie d'Emmanuel.*

Kraft, James. "Fiction as Autobiography in Québec: Notes on Pierre Vallières and Marie-Claire Blais." *Novel* 6, no. 1 (Fall 1972): 73–78. Stresses similarities between Vallières's autobiography and Blais's fictional account of a Quebec childhood in *Manuscrits de Pauline Archange*. Sees Vallières's book as making an explicitly political statement and Blais's as being concerned with the quality and dimension of human existence.

Lecker, Robert A. "The Aesthetics of Deception: Marie-Claire Blais' *A Season in the Life of Emmanuel*." *Essays on Canadian Writing* 4 (1976): 42–55. Reads *Une saison dans la vie d'Emmanuel* as the representation of a despairing poetic consciousness that creates itself within a deliberate framework of fantasy, dream, and lie.

Lewis, Paula Gilbert. "From Shattered Reflections to Female Bonding: Mirroring in Marie-Claire Blais's *Visions d'Anna*." *Québec Studies* 2 (1984): 94–104. Uses contemporary feminist theory to explore relationships between mothers and daughters in *Visions d'Anna,* as contrasted with the negative vision of this relationship in *La Belle Bête*.

—. "Les Textes dramatiques radiophoniques de Marie-Claire Blais." *Québec Studies* 10 (1990): 37–44. Analyzes five radio plays from the 1970s as an expression of women's progress toward a language that expresses their own truths and realities.

Marchand, Alain-Bernard. "*Les Manuscrits de Pauline Archange* de M.-C.Blais: Eros et Thanatos." *Voix et Images* 7, no. 2 (Winter 1982): 343–49. Sees conflicting elements of desire and death as essential to construction of *Manuscrits de Pauline Archange*.

Marcotte, Gilles. "La Dialectique de l'ancien et du nouveau chez Marie-Claire Blais, Jacques Ferron et Réjean Ducharme." *Voix et Images* 6 (Fall 1980): 63–73. Explores ambivalence of Blais's treatment of traditional Quebec values, especially in Grand-Mère Antonette.

—. "Les Enfants de Grand-Mère Antoinette." In *Le Roman à l'imparfait: Essais sur le roman québécois d'aujourd'hui,* 93–137. Montreal: La Presse, 1976. Rejecting Goldmann's sociological reading, Marcotte views Blais's work in the context of the "family romance," seeing her situations and characters as variations on the plight of the foundling child.

—. "Une entrevue avec Marie-Claire Blais: 'Je veux aller le plus loin possible.'" *Voix et Images* 8 (Winter 1983): 191–209. A sensitive interview, covering various aspects of Blais's life and work through *Manuscrits de Pauline Archange*.

Mitterand, Henri. "Coup de pistolet dans un concert: *Une saison dans la vie d'Emmanuel.*" *Voix et Images* 2 (April 1977): 407–17. Contests Goldmann's optimistic political reading of *Une saison dans la vie d'Emmanuel,* seeing it as possessing the language of blasphemy but not of political revolution.

Mowshowitz, H. H. "L'Adolescent vaincu." *Canadian Literature* 52 (Spring 1972): 48–56. Sees the major theme of *Une saison dans la vie d'Emmanuel* as adolescence, a pessimistic vision in which the adolescent is emprisoned by his milieu and the demands of a difficult life.

Nadeau, Vincent. "Des Filles et du grand méchant loup: Une lecture de *L'Ange de la solitude.*" *Québec Studies* 10 (1990): 45–50. Reflects on ambivalence of perspective on women's community in *L'Ange de la solitude.*

Parker, Douglas H. "The Shattered Glass: Mirror and Illusion in *Mad Shadows.*" *Journal of Canadian Fiction* 2, no. 4 (1973): 68–70. An analysis of the function of mirrors and mirroring in Blais's first novel.

Ramberg, Michael Lynn. "*La Belle Bête:* Contestation et monologisme." *Québec Studies* 10 (1990): 9–18. Argues that in *La Belle Bête* the monologic character of the narrative structure reinforces the patriarchal premises it tries to contest.

Ricouart, Janine. "Le Théâtre de Marie-Claire Blais." *Québec Studies* (1990): 29–36. Reads Blais's works in the context of Quebec women's theater.

Sears, Dianne. "Figures of Transgression in Marie-Claire Blais's Trilogy, *Manuscrits de Pauline Archange.*" *Québec Studies* 10 (1990): 19–28. Explores different levels of transgression embodied in Pauline Archange, especially the transgressive force of writing.

Serafin, Bruce. "Marie-Claire Blais' *La Belle Bête.*" *Essays on Canadian Writing* 7–8 (Fall 1977): 63–73. Argues against naturalistic reading of *Une saison dans la vie d'Emmanuel.*

Slama, Béatrice. "*La Belle Bête,* ou la double scène." *Voix et Images* 8 (Winter 1983): 211–28. A reading of *La Belle Bête* in its specificity as a gender-marked text, focusing on the mother-daughter relationship and the feminine rewriting of various fairy tales.

Stratford, Philip. "Portraits of the Artist: Alice Munro and Marie-Claire Blais." In *All the Polarities: Comparative Studies in Contemporary Canadian Novels in French and English,* 56–70. Toronto: ECW Press, 1986. One of the best comparative studies of English and French-Canadian literature, Stratford's book sees *Une saison dans la vie d'Emmanuel* as grounded in satire and black parody, thus relying on a process of generalization, as contrasted with Munro's emphasis on specific facts and the unique quality of experience.

Tremblay, Victor-Laurent. "L'Art de la fugue dans *Le Loup* de Marie-Claire Blais." *French Review* 59, no. 6 (May 1986): 911–20. Shows how the novel is structured by musical elements and suggests that Blais's depiction uses homosexuality to address universal human issues.

Viswanathan, Jacqueline. "Cette danse au fond des coeurs: Transparence des consciences dans *Le Sourd dans la ville* et *Visions d'Anna* de Marie-Claire Blais." *Canadian Literature* 111 (Winter 1986): 86–99. Sees originality of these novels in their narrative voice, characterized by frequent changes of focus within a continuity of tone and style.

Waelti-Walters, Jennifer. "Guilt: The Prison of This World." *Canadian Literature* 88 (Spring 1981): 47–51. Reads *L'Exécution* as a presentation of the spiritual and rational conflicts created by traditional dogma and education in the modern world, as an indictment against the Catholic Church and its hold over Quebec society.

———. "Cinderella and *Mad Shadows* (Blais)." In *Fairy Tales and the Female Imagination,* 45–57. Montreal: Eden Press, 1982. Shows how Blais uses fairy-tale motifs to expose the rigid constructs of masculinity and femininity in society.

Wilson, Edmund. "Marie-Claire Blais." In *O Canada: An American's Notes on Canadian Culture,* 147–57. New York: Noonday Press/Farrar, Straus & Giroux, 1964. Describes Blais as a writer in a class by herself, based on a reading of her first four "remarkable" novels.

Index

The Author

Mary Jean Green is professor of French and associate dean of the faculty for the humanities at Dartmouth College. She received her Ph.D. from Harvard University and is the author of *Fiction in the Historical Present: French Writers and the Thirties* (1986) and *Louis Guilloux: An Artisan of Language* (1980). She was the founding editor of the journal *Québec Studies* and a founding member of the American Council for Quebec Studies. She has served on the Executive Council of the Association for Canadian Studies in the United States and the editorial board of the *International Journal of Canadian Studies*. In 1991 she received the Donner Medal for her contributions to Canadian Studies in the United States. She is completing a book on Quebec women writers.